blue
rider
press

DAVE HILL

DOESN'T

LIVE HERE

ANYMORE

ALSO BY DAVE HILL

*Tasteful Nudes: . . . and Other Misguided Attempts
at Personal Growth and Validation*

DAVE HILL DOESN'T LIVE HERE ANYMORE

‹ · ›

DAVE HILL

BLUE RIDER PRESS

NEW YORK

blue
rider
press

An imprint of Penguin Random House LLC
375 Hudson Street
New York, New York 10014

ISBN 9780399166754

Printed in the United States of America
1   3   5   7   9   10   8   6   4   2

Book design by Meighan Cavanaugh

For my dad, Bob Hill, the best dad.

*This book is also dedicated to the memory
of Patrick Salt Ryan and Danielle Velarde.*

CONTENTS

◀ · ▶

DAVE HILL
DOESN'T
LIVE HERE
ANYMORE

PREFACE

This is a book about journeys, both physical and mental as well as emotional and spiritual. I also end up running a couple errands. I need you to be cool with that.

—Dave Hill

A BRIEF
INTRODUCTION,
OR HI, I'M DAVE

SOMETIMES YOU SIT DOWN ON A COUCH AND NEXT thing you know seven years have gone by. At least that's what happened with me anyway. But first, let's back things up a little.

Hi. How are you? I'm incredible. Thank you so much for asking. And thank you for reading my book. It is my second. I realize, however—statistically speaking, anyway—odds are decent that you haven't gotten around to reading my first book* yet, so I should probably bring you up to speed, so neither of us gets completely lost, not unlike the time my friend Kevin made me go

---

* It's called *Tasteful Nudes* and there is no rush to read it, as it is a timeless classic. Take your time—when you are ready, it will be there for you. But if you have, by chance, already read it, please don't get worked up or anything if you already know some of the stuff I'm about to tell you here in this introduction. It will be over soon enough, and then you can jump into this literary adventure with both feet.

see *Hellbound: Hellraiser II* with him, even though I hadn't seen the first Hellraiser movie.

"Why does that guy have nails for hair?" I asked him.

"Shut up," Kevin whispered. "I'm trying to watch the movie."

I was totally confused for over an hour and a half and there was nothing I could do about it because he drove.

Anyway, my name is Dave and I come from the mean streets of Cleveland,* the Paris of northeastern Ohio.† Specifically, I'm from a town called University Heights, or "the City of Beautiful Homes," as it is referred to on all the signs coming into town and I imagine on most official stationery, partly because it's true, but probably also because all the other cool town slogans were already taken.

I come from a pretty regular family, I suppose. We never wore ascots to dinners served to us by uniformed maids struggling to balance fancy silver platters or anything. And when it came time for tennis lessons, I had to take group lessons instead of getting the one-on-one attention I so desperately needed, a situation that enraged me at the time but is now something I would like to think has helped make me the man I am today, a guy who understands that when it comes time to face off against the big ball machine of life, we should each get a turn to flail away with all our might.

I spent most of my life in Cleveland and never really planned to leave because—despite Internet rumors—it's actually a pretty

---

* Technically, I'm from the suburbs, which, the more I think about it, aren't necessarily all that mean. But trust me on this one, they can get pretty irritable sometimes, which is something, and I'll take it.

† Ask anyone.

magical place, especially when you squint or blur your eyes just right. But one day back in 2003 I decided to go visit some friends in New York City and never left. You'd be surprised what you can accomplish by just setting your bag down in someone's apartment and refusing to leave.

Then my mother died, and it was back to Cleveland I went, at least for a little while anyway.

It's a strange thing when someone in your life dies. There's the sadness and grief, of course. And also the mammoth disbelief that comes with any great loss. But all of that was multiplied times roughly a billion when my mother died. I couldn't make sense of it, no matter how hard I tried and no matter how much time I might have had to prepare for it. It's as if you are standing in the middle of a highway at midnight, and way off in the distance you see an eighteen-wheeler clearing the horizon, its headlights just starting to crack the darkness and bearing down on you. You stand there watching and waiting as the truck gets closer and closer, so close that you can almost make out the license plate. And then the truck runs right over you. Still, somehow, you just lie there thinking, "Huh—I never saw that one coming." In short, it was awful.

The funeral and all that were a blur. My sister Miriam and I gave speeches.

"Keep it down to a minute or so each," the priest told us beforehand.

"Screw you, pal," I wanted to say back to him before remembering how disappointed my mother would have been if I mouthed off to a priest like that, especially on his own turf. Still, it felt warranted. My mother was at that church pretty much whenever it was unlocked, as best I could tell—the least that priest could do was let my mom's kids say whatever they wanted for as long as they wanted on her final visit. Regardless, my sister and I both ignored him altogether and spoke for as long as we felt like in honor of our mother and also to show that priest that the Hill kids are no pushovers.

The morning of the funeral, I thought back to when I was a kid, when my mom's younger sister, my aunt Betty, was sick with cancer, and my parents and I went to visit her in the hospital after one of my Pee Wee hockey games. I was still young and clueless enough to think that no matter how old or sick someone was, a quick checkup, a glass or two of orange juice, and a couple nights' rest at the hospital, and he or she would be back in action in no time. We stood in the room for about a half hour with me still in full uniform, the stink of my sweaty hockey pads giving any and all other strange hospital smells a run for their money, watching Aunt Betty struggle through dinner.

"Do you want to watch TV?"

"No."

"Are you thirsty?"

"Yes."

"Your roommate sure is quiet, huh?"

"Not enough."

You know—the usual hospital small talk.

"Aunt Betty seems like she's doing a little better today, huh?" I said to my mom as we walked back to the station wagon afterward.

"Do you know where your blazer is?" she replied, seemingly from out of nowhere.

"Why?" I asked, slightly annoyed. At the time I tended to associate wearing a blazer with doing stuff that I didn't want to do.

"Because the funeral will probably be sometime next week," she said.

My mom could be all business sometimes. It was a coping mechanism, I guess.

Back then, the blazer in question was a kelly-green sport jacket that had been handed down to me from my older brother, Bob. It made me look and even kind of feel like I'd just won the Masters, which was admittedly pretty cool in most settings, but not ideal for a funeral. "Look—it's Jack Nicklaus," some jackass would usually say whenever I wore it.

As I got dressed for my mom's funeral all those years later, it occurred to me that the outfit I'd chosen—a black suit with a green tie I'd picked out mostly in a nod to my mom's Irishness but perhaps also in an unconscious nod to that green jacket— marked the first time I'd gone to a funeral dressed entirely in clothes that hadn't been borrowed. Even better, I'd paid for them with my own money. And perhaps most impressive, I knew exactly where they were ahead of time. I smiled thinking how proud or at least not annoyed my mom would have been about all that.

Once the actual funeral part of the funeral was over with, it wasn't so bad, at least as far as unfortunate activities go, anyway. You hang out, eat and drink, and talk to people. It's kind of like a wedding, only slightly less awful in that there's almost no danger of anyone at any point asking you if you're having a good time. And for the next few weeks after that, there are cookies and sandwiches coming from every direction, and all sorts of people telling you how they, too, think it sucks that your mother died without ever using those exact words. The distraction does wonders in temporarily softening the blow. It's like a bomb that goes off, only instead of shrapnel flying everywhere, there are beautiful flowers, so many that it takes a little while to notice the gigantic hole in your chest.

As awful as losing my mom was, though, it surprisingly came with a few positive side effects. For starters, somehow in losing her, I realized we were also weirdly inseparable and, in fact, always had been. My mother's death also presented me with the opportunity to get better acquainted with my dad, this mysterious man I'd been running into down in the basement all these years. Who was he? Where did he come from? And, perhaps most important, what would our lives be like now that our middle-woman was gone and there was no one to tell us what time we'd be leaving for P.F. Chang's? And while I was at it, it was an opportunity to also learn more about who I was and how the hell I wound up sitting here writing to you in my underwear right now. I mean, sure, it's a lot of fun and my hair looks great and all. But weren't things supposed to be different?

Anyway, these are just a few of the questions I've attempted to answer in the pages that follow. And while many of the essays in this book focus on these last few years since my mother died, I also dip into my more distant and at times even sordid past to share some as-yet-untold tales, some of which have profanity, some of which do not. I go to prison,* get pizza with my dad,

---

* Again.

learn a thing or two about kung fu, and a bunch of other stuff besides that stuff. In short, this book pretty much has everything, so if you want to go ahead and throw all your other books in the trash, I'm sure as hell not going to stop you.

I hope you enjoy it so much.

MY OLD MAN
AND THE SEA

DURING MY FORMATIVE YEARS, AND PROBABLY FOR
at least a couple years after that, it was my firm belief that
if a restaurant had a commercial on television, that meant it was
among the very best of the best, home to the finest in contempo-
rary culinary offerings, the food of the gods.

Leading the pack in this category by a wide margin as far as
I was concerned was, of course, Red Lobster, the only establish-
ment brazen enough to do away altogether with shots of attractive young couples on a hot, lobster-based date and entire
families having a really great time at their restaurant in its commercials. Instead, Red Lobster made the food itself the star.
Lobster tails, unburdened from their shells and glistening with
melted butter, were baptized in slow motion by a climaxing
lemon wedge presumably squeezed by the mighty hand of Posei-
don himself. Breaded strips of succulent cod lay suggestively,
still in the very pan in which they had been so delicately braised,

mere moments away from being robbed of their innocence by a tub of tartar sauce waiting furtively among french fries still hot enough to sear human flesh. Hush puppies, popcorn shrimp— what the hell were they, anyway?* I didn't know or even care, I just wanted them in my mouth immediately.

"Can we *pleeease* go to Red Lobster?" I called to my dad in the next room immediately after one of Red Lobster's seductive spots had just aired, my eyes still glued to the TV as the address of the local franchise slowly faded from the screen.

"No," he said.

"Why?" I asked incredulously.

"Because," he replied.

It was bad enough that my request to have my bedroom re-done with purple shag carpet had recently been denied. But this latest indignity was some next-level bullshit.

"Who and what are we Hills if not people worthy to dine at Red Lobster, where delicious and freshly prepared seafood dishes are priced to move in a family-friendly environment seven days a week during lunch and dinner at any number of convenient lo-cations throughout northeastern Ohio?" I wondered, pressing my face as deep into a couch cushion as the stuffing would allow.

"I could take you fishing instead if you'd like," my dad offered, standing in the doorway of the family room moments later.

I'm not entirely sure what part of my asking to go to Red Lob-ster caused my dad to make the mental leap to suggest we go

---

* I'm still not entirely sure how popcorn shrimp is different from totally regu-lar shrimp, but I can now say with confidence that hush puppies are some kind of fried bread.

fishing instead. But these were simpler times and action in suburban Cleveland was harder to come by, so I decided not to question it and just said yes.

"Great," my dad said. "I know a good spot in Port Clinton."

Port Clinton. It sounded like the kind of place where everybody, even small children, had at least one squinty eye, smoked a pipe, and wore a woolen cap of some sort year round. Further research indicated that Port Clinton was the self-proclaimed "Walleye Capital of the World." And even further research indicated that a walleye was some kind of fish.

"I can't wait," I told him, unsure myself whether I was being sarcastic or not.

We planned our trip for the following weekend. And I guess since it qualified as a sort of male bonding–type thing, my brother, Bob, who had never shown even the slightest interest in Red Lobster or the mysteries of the sea in general up until this point, was invited along, too.

In the days leading up to the trip, my excitement grew, which, looking back on it, wasn't all that surprising, as I had, after all, come from a long line of seafaring people. My great-grandfather had been a ship captain, steering cargo along the Great Lakes for weeks at a time as his wife and children waited patiently back home in Cleveland, oblivious to the harsh realities of the angry midwestern waters he navigated unflinchingly to Michigan, Illinois, and beyond. And my grandparents had spent the last few winters in Florida, returning each spring with petrified starfish, assorted nautical-themed knickknackery, and tales of shuffleboard games and other water-adjacent contests that kept my siblings and me rapt for hours. The more I thought about it, the more I realized that fishing was in my blood, maybe even more so than eating at Red Lobster, where, it was my understanding, they "sea food differently."

"We'll have to leave here tomorrow at six a.m.," my dad announced the night before our journey.

"Why?" I asked.

"We want to get there while the fish are still biting," he explained.

I didn't quite understand what some fish had to do all day besides sit there waiting for me to lodge a rusty hook in his gullet. But since my dad had apparently done this before and had the cool fishing hat to prove it, I decided to just roll with it.

The following morning, my brother and I piled into our Plymouth station wagon, groggy and still a bit confused, and my dad drove us to Port Clinton, which sat about eighty miles west of our suburban home in a territory of Ohio as yet unspoiled by the fast-paced energy of Cleveland or the glitz and glamour of Toledo.

Shortly after sunup, my brother and I were shaken from our slumber by the sound of the car's tires hitting a gravel parking lot at the edge of Lake Erie, where fishermen types readied their boats along a wooden dock for a long day of drinking. We stumbled out of our station wagon.

"You here for the charter boat?" asked an old fireplug of a man who, with his long gray beard and pipe and all, was really delivering on my expectation of what the average Port Clintonian might look like.

"No," my dad told him.

"You sure?" he asked with a look that suggested we were completely out of our minds if we didn't get on his boat posthaste. "I guarantee you'll catch a lot of fish."

"No, thank you," my dad said, a bit more forcefully this time, as we continued past him toward a bait shop at the edge of the dock.

"What's a charter boat?" I asked along the way.

"It's a boat where they take you out fishing," my dad said.

"Shouldn't we do that, then?" I asked.

"No," my dad said.

"Why?" I asked.

"Because *I'm* taking you fishing," he explained.

"But can you *guarantee* we'll catch fish like that guy just did?" I asked.

"No," he said.

"Sounds like we should probably get on that charter boat, then, huh?" I said.

My dad pretended not to hear me after that, but it didn't matter because as soon as we entered the bait shop I was transfixed. Hooks, lures, worms at least twice as long and fat as any I had ever seen in my entire life before—they were everywhere, lining every inch of the place, as far as the eye could see. For a kid who had only a couple days earlier convinced himself and at least a couple other kids in the neighborhood he'd been born to fish, it felt like a homecoming of sorts.

"I'll take two tubs of worms, please," my dad said to another guy with a beard slumped over the counter, like he'd been standing in the exact same spot since the Korean War let out.

The guy grunted a couple times before pushing two small plastic containers, the kind one might use for potato salad or some other fun side dish, across the counter toward my dad. My dad grunted a couple times back at the guy before pushing some cash toward him and handing my brother and me each a container of worms to carry back to the car.

As soon as I slid into the backseat, I opened the container of worms in my lap, dug into the cold, damp dirt the color of crushed Oreos the worms had been packed in, and pulled one out for inspection. It was massive and stretched out like an especially gross Slinky as I held it in the air. I was just about to make a suggestive yet ultimately humorous joke by momentarily dangling the worm just below my crotch when my dad made eye contact with me through the rearview mirror.

"Don't play with the worms, David," he said.

"Yeah, don't play with the worms," my brother chimed in.

"I'm just getting them ready," I explained.

"Ready for what?" Bob asked.

"Death," I said.

"Just put the worms away, all right?" my dad said, pulling out of the parking lot.

We drove for a mile or so before my dad pulled to the side of the road alongside an inlet.

"Here we are," he said, cutting off the engine and staring out at the water. "I've got a good feeling about this spot."

As we grabbed the fishing tackle from the back of the car along with a bag of Cheetos, a tube of sunscreen, and a few cans of Dr Pepper we'd brought along with us in a cooler, I imagined this must have been exactly like what previous generations of Hills had done fifty, sixty—who knows—maybe even a hundred years before. It was awesome.

After we settled on the bank, my dad baited our fishhooks and handed a rod each to my brother and me. I stood there watching the worm writhe on my hook momentarily, its mysterious worm innards spilling out from where it had been punctured, before my dad began explaining to us what casting was and how exactly we might go about doing that. And while it took a few tries to get all of our lines into the water instead of a nearby tree or our hair, eventually, with some assistance from my dad,* it happened.

And then we waited.

And waited.

"How long before we catch a fish?" I asked my dad, breaking the silence after what felt like hours but was more likely a minute or two.

"I don't know," my dad said. "We might have to wait a while."

"How long is that, you think?" I asked.

"Stop talking, David," my brother Bob said. "You're gonna scare the fish away!"

"Maybe you are," I said.

"No, I'm not," he said.

"Well, maybe I'm not, either," I replied.

After I got done pretty much owning my brother like that, the three of us turned our attention back to the cruel, murky waters of Lake Erie, the most unforgiving of all the Great Lakes, as far as I was concerned at the time.

"Do you think the fish like Cheetos?" I asked my dad a couple minutes later.

"Not historically," he said.

----

* Which is to say he eventually just grabbed our rods from us and cast our lines into the water himself.

"Can we at least see if they might want some?" I asked.

"Shut up, David!" my brother groaned, this time elbowing me in the ribs for emphasis. "You're scaring the fish again!"

And then I was all like, "No, I'm not," and elbowed him back.

And then he was all like, "Yeah, you are!" and elbowed me a second time.

And then I was all like, "Well, maybe *you* are," only that time I intentionally *didn't* elbow him just to mess with his head.

It pretty much went like that or at least some variation of that for the next couple hours. Occasionally it would be decided that one of our worms had lost its will to live and my dad would wrap a fresh one onto our hooks if for no other reason than to get my brother or me to stop complaining that our worms "sucked." During this time, none of us even got so much as a nibble. We were about to pack it in for the day when suddenly, against all odds, I felt a tug on my line.

"Dad!" I chirped. "I think I got a fish!"

"No, you don't," my brother said dismissively.

"Yes, I do!" I said as my fishing rod began slowly bending down toward the water.

"It looks like you do," my dad agreed.

"You got a fish! You got a fish!" my brother screamed, quickly changing his tune and jumping on the "Dave has a fish" bandwagon.

"Stop screaming!" I told him. "You'll scare the fish."

And then Bob was all like, "No, I won't!"

And so I was just like, "Yeah, you will!"

And then he was all like, "Maybe *you* will!" even though that didn't even make sense, really, since, given the fact that I had already lodged a hook in the fish's mouth and was now trying to remove it from its life source, I was probably already scaring it plenty, the more I sit here thinking about it right now.

Meanwhile, my dad had set his fishing rod down in the grass and walked over to help me with mine.

"Easy does it," he said, leaning over my shoulder like he was about to help me perfect my golf swing. "Now, slo-o-o-o-wly start reeling it in."

I expected a battle of *The Old Man and the Sea* proportions to ensue, just me and perhaps the biggest fish ever to be pulled from Lake Erie duking it out as people began running from every corner of town to catch a glimpse of the hot fishing action going on right in their own backyard before the story was inevitably handed over to legend and repeated ad nauseam at every campfire, Rotary Club meeting, and plasma donor waiting room within a hundred miles of the place.

"What do you think it is?" I asked my dad. "A swordfish? A hammerhead, maybe?"

"Anything is possible," my dad said, just trying to be supportive.

"It might be a walleye or a trout," my brother added, pulling things into perspective.

Whatever it was, as best I could tell, it seemed to be looking to get the whole thing over with more than anything else. Aside from a few halfhearted, last-ditch attempts at plunging deeper into the water, the beast on my line put up about as much fight as I imagine a damp sock might. And when I finally pulled it from the water, instead of the handsome, silvery specimen glistening in the sun I'd anticipated, I saw a sad, armor-plated mass the color of sewage hanging limply on my line. Was it a fish, the missing link, or something else entirely?

"Looks like you got yourself a catfish," my dad said, clearing up matters.

"Cool," I replied.

I admittedly had no idea what my dad was talking about. And frankly the fish's barbels* were scaring me. But even so, a fish was a fish as far as I was concerned, so it felt like a triumph no matter what.

"Shall we head home with him?" my dad asked, hoping to wrap things up.

"Yeah!" I replied.

It felt like a long day already, so my brother, though fishless, went along with the plan, too. After my dad dislodged the hook from the catfish's gaping maw and dumped him into our cooler along with some water and a few leftover Dr Peppers, we began the schlep back to Cleveland. While my brother Bob called shotgun, I stayed in the back with the cooler, lifting the lid every few seconds to make sure my catch wasn't plotting an escape or anything. And as I did so, I felt like a man, a real man whose proclivity for the arts and disdain for team sports was something my family had no reason to worry about whatsoever. It was an exhilarating feeling to be sure. At least for a few miles anyway.

As we got back on the highway and Lake Erie began to drift from sight, I was overcome with a strange feeling. Was I carsick? Or somehow homesick, even though I was actually with my fam-

---

* Barbels are those creepy whisker-like appendages catfish have protruding from the face and head area. I just looked it up.

ily? I couldn't quite pinpoint it, so I just waited for the feeling to go away as my dad, my brother, and I began to discuss the various ways we might prepare my big catch for dinner that night.

"We could grill him," my dad said.

"Or we could fry him," Bob suggested.

"We could even steam him," my dad continued. "I like a steamed fish."

"Yeah," I said with a shrug. "I guess any of those would work fine."

It was then that I realized I kind of felt bad for the little guy. Earlier that day, he had been minding his own business, presumably bottom-feeding his way along the floor of the mighty Lake Erie without a care in the world. Now he was mere hours away from being knocked unconscious, skinned alive, cooked on our stove top, and served up at our dinner table alongside some hastily made coleslaw, where he would inevitably be rejected after a few bites at best, before my siblings and I lobbied to be taken to McDonald's or one of its nearby competitors instead.

I tried to power through my misgivings about dragging the ray-finned* bastard back to our place, but a few miles later they became more than even I, this young yet still reasonably hardened salt, could handle.

"Stop the car," I all of a sudden squealed to my dad, leaning over the front seat.

"Are you gonna puke?" Bob asked.

"Probably, but that's not it," I said. "Right now I just wanna put this fish back in the lake."

---

* This is another cool fact about catfish I just looked up.

"You don't want to have him for dinner?" my dad asked.

"No," I replied. "I don't want *anyone* to have him for dinner."

I must have sounded pretty convincing, because next thing I knew my dad pulled off the highway and began steering us back north toward the water, no questions asked. We didn't go all the way back to where I'd caught the catfish, but as my dad dumped the little guy back in the water, he assured me the fish would take it from there, eventually tracking down his friends and family and getting back to whatever fish bullshit catfish like him tend to get up to.

To his credit, my brother didn't give me any crap about setting the catfish free when we got back in the car. Sure, an implied "You are a wuss, Dave" hung in the air, but it only lasted a few exits at best.

We pulled into our driveway back in University Heights an hour or so later, worn out and weary (well, at least I was, anyway).

"How did the fishing go?" my mom asked once we got inside. "You catch anything?"

"David did," Bob said.

"Oh, yeah?" my mom said, smiling. "Where is it?"

"We threw him back," my dad said.

"Why?" my mom asked.

"He was a pretty big fish, big enough for most fishermen in fact," my dad explained, "but he just wasn't big enough for David."

"Yeah," I agreed. "You know I only like to catch the really, really big ones."

"Of course, Davey," my mom said, going along with the story. "Of course."

We never went fishing together again after that day. And while a handful of my buddies began to go fishing regularly by the time we were all teenagers, I was rarely invited along because it was decided that I "talk too much" and "might scare the fish."

As for Red Lobster, though, I finally made that dream come true by joining a handful of friends on a recent outing to the franchise's bustling Times Square location. It was admittedly not as glamorous and inviting as the commercials from my youth had promised. And while I did my best to power through the Ultimate Feast®, which—to be fair—looked really great in all the pictures, it left me with force mere moments after I got off the subway later that night.

Sometimes I worry I'm just not cut out for the sea, after all.

TRAVELING MEN

IT WAS A FEW DAYS AFTER MY MOM'S FUNERAL THAT I fell out of bed, pulled on the nearest pair of pants, and headed downstairs to the kitchen to find my dad sitting at the table, eating toast and flipping through the *Cleveland Plain Dealer*, the local paper of record. The house was already alive with the usual cacophony of mysterious beeping noises—a microwave that had finished reheating coffee for the third time here, a cell phone loaded with messages my dad wasn't entirely sure how to access with confidence there, and other things of unknown origin, most of which seemed to be operating at a frequency my dad either couldn't or chose not to hear, as he seemed completely unfazed by all of them. As for me, they drove me completely bonkers. It was as if we were under relentless attack by a plague of mechanical locusts. And there was no defeating them. As soon as I tracked down the cell phone under a couch cushion, a smoke detector with a dying battery would take over from the second floor as if on cue, like every electronic device in the place was conspiring to slowly chip away at my sanity. It was my own private hell.

"There's coffee in the machine if you want it," my dad offered as I righted myself in the doorway.

"Full strength?" I asked.

"No," he answered. "Half-caff."

I'm still not sure whether he bought it that way or if it was his own diabolical creation, but "half-caff," as the name hints, was a mix of regular and decaffeinated coffee that my dad had taken to drinking the past few years, presumably in an effort to stay only half-awake. It was too noncommittal for me, though, and I refused to drink it. I don't think I ever saw him actually drink it, either. As best I could tell, he'd brew up a pot every morning, pour himself a cup, reheat it in the microwave half an hour later, eventually remember he'd left his coffee in the microwave about a half hour after that, reheat it again, and repeat the whole cycle over and over until sometime in the afternoon, when either the coffee had evaporated entirely or he'd maybe decided it was too late in the day to drink coffee, whichever came first.

But even though my dad had to have been aware of my disdain for "half-caff" at this point, he'd still offer me a cup of coffee most mornings whenever I was home anyway. And I'd ask what kind of coffee it was every time, even though I already knew the answer. Then he'd reply as if the answer might somehow be different from the day before. It was our daily ritual, a ritual that usually ended with me heading up to the corner to get a regular cup of coffee. It was as if we were part of a secret society, and without having this conversation at the start of each day, our meetings couldn't officially come to order.

"I'll be back in a few minutes," I said to my dad as I grabbed my mom's old key ring* off the counter and headed for the door.

"Okay," he replied, turning his attention back to the toast.

As I shuffled out back toward the car, I thought about how many times I'd found my mother just sitting there in the driveway, parked in the very same spot, while I was growing up. I'd hear the hum of the car pulling into the driveway and then listen for the sound of the car door finally opening and her getting out. Sometimes she'd sit there for a full twenty minutes before coming back into the house. It was almost like a performance art piece, something Marina Abramović or even Tilda Swinton, the great box sleeper, might attempt if they were low on options. As a kid, I naturally assumed my mom did this simply because she was losing her mind, but now, for the first time, it occurred to me that maybe the reason she waited so long to go back into the house was because she knew there were five young kids waiting for her inside, each with their own list of demands for food, cash, permission to go to a friend's house, or—perhaps worst of all—attention. The more I thought about it, the more impressed I was that she ever pulled back into the driveway in the first place.

---

* Years ago, one of my mom's friends decided to have my mom's name, Bunny, carved out of a block of wood into an unwieldy key holder about an inch wide and six inches long. Between that and the electronic door opener that also hung from the key ring, it not only was hard to miss but—when placed in my front pants pocket—sent a message I was uncomfortable with.

A couple minutes later, I rolled up to Fairmount Circle, the shopping center up the street from our house. For most of my youth, Fairmount Circle was an oasis, a beacon of possibilities, where I could load up on candy, maybe run into a girl I thought might tolerate me, or even come head-to-head with a nun from school who had been rendered powerless (at least to my mind, anyway) by leaving both school and church grounds.

Fairmount Circle had all the usual shopping center stuff—a grocery store, a pharmacy, a barbershop,* a restaurant, and whatever else. When I was a kid, I'd steal money from my mother's purse or—perhaps more accurately—borrow money without her really caring and walk up there to buy as much candy and

---

* Like just about every guy in my neighborhood, the barbershop at Fairmount Circle was the place I would go to get the exact same short-and-parted-to-the-side haircut that everyone else got there unless they asked to have their hair shaved off altogether. When I was a kid, it drove me nuts. I'd see pictures of Kiss or Foghat or anyone with long hair, really, and dream of having sweet rock hair like them as I avoided having to go to the barber for as long as possible. Then, every couple months, I'd be forced to sit down in a chair in that barbershop and be made to look like every other kid in the neighborhood, like some guy you'd never even see in the audience at a Foghat concert much less in the actual band. I'm sorry both to you, the reader, and the members of Foghat for dragging them into this, but hopefully you see my point.

When I was in high school and old enough to both drive and make my own hair care decisions, I heard a commercial for some salon on the other side of town that had the Smiths playing in the background and I knew it was my chance to break free from the tyranny of the barbershop at Fairmount Circle. There, a phalanx of goths and other local misfits who just so happened to kind of, sort of know how to cut hair were waiting to destroy my head. And who cares if they usually made me look like I was the merch guy for a Flock of Seagulls tribute band? It was my way of letting everyone in my town know that I was different, that I wasn't one of them, that I wasn't going along with the plan. I hope it worked.

pop* as my heist† would allow. Occasionally, with bated breath and fingers crossed, I'd take a stroll down the magazine aisle at the pharmacy in hopes that someone had mistakenly left an issue of *Playboy*‡ on one of the lower shelves where I could reach it without anyone noticing that an elementary school student was up to no good. This was in simpler times, the days before both the Internet and shrink wrapping, when a kid like me still had a fighting chance of having his dreams come true right then and there in aisle three. Of course, it never actually happened, but I

---

* I'm from the Midwest. This is what we call soda when we talk amongst ourselves.

† On days when my mother's purse was nowhere to be found, I'd usually resort to paying for things with returnable bottles, a popular form of currency in my youth. In the wintertime, my buddy John and I used to hide returnable bottles in the piles of snow left by the plows in the parking lot across the street from Fairmount Circle. It was our secret stash that we'd use to pay for stuff whenever neither of us managed to pilfer any spare change from our mothers' purses. We'd made a pact that we'd never turn in the bottles for money unless we were together, too, but somewhere along the line, one of us—I can't remember who—must have been bragging around the neighborhood about our treasure trove, because one cold winter day we discovered all of the bottles we had so carefully hidden had suddenly vanished.

"We've been hit," I told John, up to my elbows in snow as I frantically searched for the bottles, some of them worth almost a quarter.

"Fuck," he said.

"Fuck is right," I said.

"Are you fucking sure?"

"Fuck yeah, I'm sure."

Neither of us could get away with much swearing at home, so our trips to the corner together were a good time to practice or at least get it out of our system during our early years. It made us feel alive.

‡ It's worth noting that as I write this, *Playboy* has just announced it will no longer feature naked pictures in its pages. Is there any reason to wander into the woods again?

didn't let that stop me from trying. It was a numbers game as far as I was concerned. And until I was old enough to drive and able to scope out other places with magazine racks, it was the faint promise of exactly that sort of action that kept me coming back to Fairmount Circle whenever possible.

"Someday somebody is gonna slip up and put that *Playboy* on the bottom shelf," young Dave thought. "And that's when I strike."

Today, though, most of that excitement was gone, and my needs had become much simpler, so once I got to the coffee shop, I ordered a large coffee and a Russian tea biscuit the size of an adult human foot to go. And as I stood there adding milk and too much sugar at the end of the counter, I spotted my old high school English teacher, Mr. Donnelly, at a corner table, typing like the wind on his laptop; some girl* I went to elementary school with corralling what appeared to be her human child; and even one of those nuns referenced earlier, all scattered across the coffee shop. It was kind of like an episode of *This Is Your Life*, a television show I have only heard about and have never actually seen but have decided to reference here anyway.

In keeping with the *This Is Your Life* theme, I ran into Mrs. Grady, the mother of at least five or six kids with whom I went to grade school, as I headed for the door.

"Hi, Mrs. Grady," I said, my voice squeaking a bit, like I was still navigating puberty. For whatever reason, whenever I run into people from my youth, I return in my mind to the age I was when

---

* Now technically a woman!

I knew them best. I'm sure there is some really good psychological explanation for this, but I bet I don't want to hear it.

"Hi, Dave," she said. "I'm sorry to hear about your mom."

"Me too," I said.

"You must miss her," she replied.

"Yeah," I told her. "But all the people swinging by the house to say hello and bring my dad and me cookies and other delicious food have been giving us great comfort."

"Oh," Mrs. Grady said, "maybe I could stop by with something later."

"Sure," I told her. "You know, if you want."

"Okay," she said, "give my best to your dad."

"Of course," I replied.

I was getting pretty good at conversations like this. And when they went just right, someone would be pulling up to the side door to drop off a Pyrex dish full of something or other within the hour. Sure, part of me felt a little guilty, but then I'd just think of that saying about lemons, try to find some extra room in the fridge, and get on with my day.

On the short drive home, it suddenly dawned on me that possibly the one good thing about my mom's being gone—at least as far as my dad was concerned, anyway—was that now he could do pretty much whatever he wanted whenever he wanted, 24/7. This isn't to say that my mom had him on lockdown during their years together or anything. It's just that with any couple, there can be a lot of moving parts, too many things that have to happen or at least be discussed five, six, or even twelve times before anything else can happen: an iron has to be checked and then possibly double- and triple-checked to make sure it's unplugged and no longer capable of starting a raging fire that burns the house to the ground the moment you walk out the door; a letter must be sealed and stamped for the last mail pickup of the day, even though that already happened; one last trip to the bathroom has to be made "just in case"; and on down the list. Next thing you know, even a simple drive to Akron can take weeks, even months of planning. Add five kids to the mix and you're lucky if you ever make it past the front lawn again.

Anyway, despite being a rather cultured and sophisticated man, at least as far as dads on our block went, my dad somehow never got around to leaving the country much, aside from my parents' honeymoon in the U.S. Virgin Islands* and the occasional drive to lower Ontario when he still had the wanderlust. But he did spend a year and a half in Japan during his stint in the Army after college, and it was something he remembered fondly.

"One night a bunch of my fellow officers and I spent the night having dinner and drinks at a geisha house," he'd recall pretty much whenever anyone anywhere even mentioned Japan or anything even remotely Asian, for that matter. "We were each paired off with a geisha, and even though mine couldn't speak a word of English and I couldn't speak a word of Japanese, we still managed to have a lovely time."

"I'll bet you did," I usually thought.

It was fun to think the worst whenever he told that story, but my dad was always quick to point out that nothing unsavory

---

* Technically not really leaving the country if you think about it, since it's still a U.S. territory.

(which is to say awesome) ever happened between him and the geisha.

"It was a perfectly respectful evening," he'd say. "Not all geishas are prostitutes, you know."

Given how well I know the guy, I unfortunately have no choice but to take him at his word on this. Still, it's fun to pretend otherwise when things get slow.

As for me, I visited Japan for the first time myself a handful of years ago and, wholesome geisha aside, got at least as big a kick out of it as my dad seemed to, so the thought of us going there together seemed like just about the greatest idea of all time. My dad could see how much the place had changed since he'd been there and I could simply pick up where I left off, giggling uncontrollably all the way as we tried out one choice phrase after another from the English-to-Japanese translation book I had borrowed and failed to return to my friend Doug on whomever happened to be standing directly in front of us at the time.

"あなたは素晴らしいダンサーです,"* my dad or I could say to some lucky Japanese person.

"見かけは、ハンサムな紳士、ありがとうございます,"† he or she would reply.

It would be just great. For everyone.

When I got back to the house, I heard a few clanks and rattling sounds coming from the basement, which meant my dad was down there doing God knows what with who knows what, so I made my way to the top of the stairs and yelled down to him.

---

* "You are a fantastic dancer."

† "Thank you for noticing, handsome gentleman."

"Hey, Dad," I said, "what do you think about the idea of you and me going on a trip to Japan together?"

"Oh," my dad replied, taking a break from making stuff clank and rattle, "that would be kind of neat."

As he said it, the look in his eyes suggested that in that moment it had dawned on him for the very first time the exact same thing I was thinking about in the car, that he was no longer part of a team, that he no longer had to discuss the idea of doing something with another person before doing it—he could just go ahead and do it. He didn't even have to yell across the entire house that he'd be back in twenty minutes or anything. He could just grab his coat and head out the door like it was no big deal at all.

"Great," I said. "I'll start looking into plane tickets."

The idea of my dad and me just hopping on a plane and making Japan our bitch together was thrilling to me, especially since I couldn't remember the last time he and I went more than a few miles away from the house together, just the two of us. A trip to Japan would be a real adventure, something most residents of northeastern Ohio probably couldn't imagine even in their wildest dreams, what with how you can arrange to drink a latte with a cat or even buy a pair of used underwear from a vending machine over there without even having to wander into the wrong section of town. We could rediscover a whole other world together, see some mind-blowing sights, and get to know each other in ways we never had before. It would be like our very own version of *Thelma and Louise*, only without the suicide pact and hopefully with him paying for everything, too. I couldn't wait.

The next day, though, my dad had a change of heart.

"You know, I was thinking about this Japan trip," he said,

"and it occurred to me that it would be pretty hard to track down any of my old friends from back when I lived there, so I don't know how much sense it makes to go."

My dad is a really smart guy, maybe even the smartest guy I've ever known, but suddenly I couldn't help but question all that.

"Are you kidding me!?" I wanted to ask him before muttering something more along the lines of "Oh, okay," and settling into his Barcalounger.

I was the tiniest bit insulted that my dad seemed to think that hanging out in Japan with his own son might not be enough entertainment in itself, that he had to catch up with "old friends" to make that ridiculously long plane trip worthwhile. I mean, don't get me wrong, I kind of wanted to see how time had treated that geisha he had told me about, too, but I also figured we could meet all-new geishas while we were there, maybe even ones without hang-ups.

A couple days later, though, my dad came to his senses.

"You know, I was thinking some more about this Japan trip," he told me, "and maybe it doesn't matter if I'm able to track down old friends while I'm there or not."

"Duh," I said.

"Excuse me?" my dad replied.

"I said I'll start looking for plane tickets again," I told him.

But before I had even had a chance to steal our neighbor's WiFi and search for flights again, my dad went ahead and rethought the Japan idea a second time, ultimately deciding it was too far away and he'd most likely be riddled with jet lag the whole time if we went there. I was disappointed, but I totally got where he was coming from. When you fly halfway around the planet like that, the jet lag is so bad that you practically begin to hallucinate, and even the basics, like wearing pants or not playing games with the sushi conveyor belt like the restaurant manager keeps asking you, start to feel like too much to handle. Usually the excitement of being somewhere new helps me power through, but I could see how that might not do the trick when you're old enough to remember a time when airline pilots helped with the luggage.

"What about Italy?" I suggested, just trying to keep the conversation going. He had never been, but I had, and figured he'd love it.

"I don't know," he said. "We'd have to walk around so much to see the Colosseum and all that stuff. It seems like a lot."

"They've got postcards for that," I told him. "We can just hang out and stuff our faces all day. They have pizza and spaghetti there, all the stuff we love."

"Hmmm. What about London?" he countered.

The flight from Cleveland to London isn't bad at all. And, as an added bonus, you even get to hang out at JFK for a couple hours along the way, at no additional charge to you or your loved ones. But the London idea didn't last long, either, because, when it gets right down to it, if you want to hang out in a gray and rainy environment for a little while, Cleveland has already got you covered.

We continued to discuss the idea of taking a trip somewhere together for a little while after that, slowly narrowing our search to places closer and closer to our house with each consecutive conversation before finally deciding to just jump in the car and go to Panera for the time being. It was a bit of a letdown, but after my dad assured me there were plenty of "international" items on the menu, it seemed crazy not to just say yes and start looking for the car keys again.

"Mind if I drive?" my dad asked as we headed out to the car a while later. "I like to stay in practice."

I didn't really mind, because if he drove, it meant that I was officially in control of the radio, so I tossed him the keys and we began the trek to Panera, which, for the record, my dad had become a real sucker for, I think mostly because it was close to the house. As for me, at the risk of upsetting their board of directors and also my dad, I'm not exactly crazy about the place—they're a little too into serving things in edible bowls, if you ask me. The way I see it, if I'm still hungry after I finish my soup, I don't need to go after the dishes—I can just ask my dad to cough up his Panera gift card and I can order some more food.

After a short drive,* we pulled into the parking lot and headed inside.

"Do you have half-caff coffee?" my dad asked some teenager in a coffee-stained apron as we bellied up to the counter.

"No," the kid answered in a manner that suggested that life, or at least Panera, was starting to beat him down. "We got regular and decaf."

"You mean you *have* regular and decaf," my dad corrected him.

"That's what I just said," the kid mumbled back.

It was nice to see Panera wasn't putting up with any of my dad's "half-caff" crap, either.

---

* Which, for the record, was jam-packed with scorching hot tunes I had dialed in for us on the car stereo without even really trying. Dokken, Blue Oyster Cult, even a little Molly Hatchet—somehow I managed to find it all, and it was awesome.

WITH BELLS ON

IT WAS THE TURN OF THE MILLENNIUM AND I WAS HEADED to New York City for what I hoped would be an action-packed weekend when I learned that all the spare couches I had planned on occupying were suddenly "taken." Before I had a chance to start reading into things, though, my brother, Bob, had an idea.

"You should give my friend Joan a call," he suggested. "You'd like her."

"Who the hell is Joan?" I asked, not exactly sure where this was headed.

"She's in her seventies," Bob explained. "Maybe you can stay with her."

I was a little confused. And naturally my inner man-child became momentarily concerned that Bob had become the kingpin of some weird geriatric good-times ring. But I was relieved to learn that Joan was a perfectly normal member of an activist group my brother belonged to at the time that would hold meetings at Joan's apartment on the Upper West Side because it could easily accommodate a throng of people looking to get worked up about things together. The place was apparently huge, a sprawling four-bedroom in a prewar building on Ninety-Eighth Street. And though the building was slowing going condo, Joan had been there for nearly thirty years and had the ridiculously cheap lease to prove it.

In recent years, Joan had begun running an informal bed-and-breakfast out of the place, an evidently illegal but common practice in New York in the days before Airbnb and other operations designed to let total strangers rifle through your things. It sounded a little strange to my midwestern ears, but not in a way I feared might end up with my skin being used to make a dress or anything, so I decided to give her a ring.

"I'm Bob Hill's brother," I told Joan over the phone.

"Bob who?" she asked.

"Bob Hill!" I shouted, suddenly remembering my brother had warned me that Joan's hearing was somewhere in the ballpark of not great and nonexistent. "He said! You might!! Have!!! A room!!!! For rent!!!!!"

"Oh," Joan replied, apparently taking a beat to really think about it. "Sure. I guess that would be fine."

Her informality was refreshing. But it also had me wondering whether she might forget our conversation altogether and immediately call the cops upon my arrival a couple days later. If that happened, though, then the cops would give me a place to stay, I reasoned, so I really couldn't lose.

I showed up outside Joan's apartment that Friday evening,

duffel bag in hand, having been waved upstairs by the doorman before I could even get her name out. The front door was unlocked and cracked open just enough to reveal a front hall bathed in candlelight. I tried the formal approach by ringing her doorbell a few times. But when that got me nowhere, I just walked right in.

"Hello?" I called out, craning my neck in that way people do when they're trying to look innocent or concerned rather than just plain thieving. "Joan?"

Given Joan's iffy aural faculties, I anticipated our first meeting was about to involve her being unable to hear me before she all of a sudden spotted some strange man standing in the middle of her apartment and began screaming bloody murder.

And I was totally right about that.

"Oh, God!!!" Joan shrieked, slapping her palm to her chest like Fred Sanford as she rounded the corner to discover me standing in her living room. "You sc-scared m-me!"

"S-sorry!" I replied, admittedly a little shaken myself.

"Just give me a moment to catch my breath," Joan said, clutching the door frame with her other hand.

I always thought of that as more of an expression, but when Joan actually stood there gasping for air for a full minute afterward, I realized she wasn't messing around.

"Are you Bob's brother?" she finally asked after getting a bit of oxygen into her lungs.

"Yes, I'm Dave," I answered.

"Hi, David," she said. "I'm Joan."

I liked that Joan instantly decided to address me by my full first name, something women a generation or more older than I tend to do for some reason, even after I tell them my name is Dave. I think it makes me sound thoughtful and sensitive, like I might excel at origami, be able to identify rare birds, or have an even rarer heart condition that kept me indoors while all the other kids played outside throughout my youth. It's kind of nice.

"A pleasure to meet you," I told her, leaning forward to offer a gentle handshake, like I was Shrek or something. "I guess you didn't hear the bell."

Short and kind of frail, Joan wore dark slacks with a brown sweater and a silk scarf around her neck, a look those women's magazines I've never read might describe as "casually elegant." And though her hair was gray and her face had the usual lines of a woman in her seventies, she was clearly beautiful, the kind of woman that, were she closer to my age, might cause me to stutter or simply excuse myself altogether unless I had enough scotch in me to hold my ground.

As for Joan's apartment, it was like stepping into an old Woody Allen movie: wood floors covered in Oriental rugs, ceilings high enough to accommodate a young giraffe, and everything a different shade of brown.

"Can I get you some tea?" she asked, turning toward the kitchen.

I wasn't much of a tea drinker, but I said yes anyway, and Joan threw a pot on the stove.

As we sat at her kitchen table waiting for the water to boil, I noticed a phalanx of used tea bags drying on the countertop. I was relieved when Joan grabbed a fresh one from the cupboard when it came time to pour my cup.

"Oh, you don't have to do that," I said, pretending to fight it.

"You're a guest," she explained. "Guests get new tea bags."

"Your house, your rules," I told her, shaking my head as if I had officially just "seen it all."

A few minutes later, Joan showed me to my room, which felt like it was a mile or two away, past the maid's quarters, the living room, the dining room, and the den—each one of them bigger than most of my New York friends' entire apartments—and down a darkened hallway all the way on the other side of the place. The room had thick shag carpeting and a queen-size bed covered in at least a dozen blankets. In the corner sat an ancient exercise bike, which, like most home exercise bikes I've encountered, moonlighted as a hanger.

"Those belonged to Donald," she told me, noting the pile of old sport coats and dress shirts draped over the handles.

As I soon learned, Donald was Joan's old boyfriend. They'd lived here together, just the two of them, until he died in a plane crash in 1980. Twenty years later, she was "just starting to figure out what to do with all his stuff."

I felt conflicted as I wondered whether Donald was my size.

"There's a key for you on the table by the front door," Joan told me. "And I'll leave some breakfast for you on the kitchen table in the morning."

"Great," I said, promising myself I wouldn't inquire about Donald's measurements at least until the next day.

Then I set my bag down at the foot of the bed and told Joan I was going for a walk around the neighborhood.

"Here," Joan said, holding up what appeared to be an old

shoelace with a half dozen tiny sleigh bells attached. "If you could ring these a few times when you come back in, that would be very helpful."

Apparently, the frequency of the bells was high enough for Joan to pick up on from across the apartment. And by ringing them upon my return, I could avoid scaring the crap out of either one of us again. It made me feel a bit like a house cat no longer able to skulk around the place undetected, but not necessarily in a bad way. In fact, the more I thought about it, ringing the bells might even be kind of fun.

"Sure thing," I told her, slipping them into my coat pocket.

"No," Joan explained. "You don't have to carry the bells around the city with you, only when you come back in the apartment."

I was a little disappointed, sure, but I set the bells on the table by the front door before heading out anyway.

"This way the bells have a chance to stay special," I told myself.

I ended up heading downtown to meet some friends after leaving Joan's place, so by the time I returned, it was already pretty late and Joan had apparently already retired to her room, as the entire place was darkened, save for a couple of candles in the hallway. I rang the tiny sleigh bells for a while anyway, just to be safe, and they delivered on their promise of being at least a little bit fun. Between that and the spooky candles, I felt kind of like a ghost, a ghost walking the halls of an apartment that seemed frozen in time somewhere around when they launched the original Broadway production of *Evita*.

As I settled into bed a few minutes later, it occurred to me what a nice change of pace it was, having my own room somewhere instead of crashing with friends downtown or with my brother, who lived a world away in the Bronx. I could come and go as I pleased and no longer felt obligated to invite whomever I was staying with everywhere I went. If I wanted to hit the batting cages at Chelsea Piers, for example, I could just reserve a cage for one and be done with it. And if I wanted to maybe swing by Anthropologie just to see what was new, I could do so without judgment. I'm sure my brother and friends enjoyed not having to worry about keeping me entertained or having me eat everything in the fridge before inevitably clogging the toilet (my trademark), too.

"If either of those things happen here," I thought, "I could probably make the problem go away with a little extra cash."

When I woke in the morning, I discovered Joan had slipped a note under my door reminding me to take advantage of the "breakfast" part of her "bed-and-breakfast," so I pulled on some clothes and shambled to the kitchen, where I discovered a cellophane-covered plate with a few cold cuts and cheese slices sitting on the table. Next to it sat a hard-boiled egg in one of those fancy little cups designed to hold exactly that sort of thing. As Joan had outlined in the note, I could make myself some toast if the mood struck, and I would find a cup of orange juice, also covered in cellophane, it turned out, in the fridge. If I wanted to have tea again, I could keep things fancy and help myself to another brand-new bag from the cupboard.

"Egg, toast, orange juice, and tea—check," I thought. The plate full of cold cuts and cheese, on the other hand, struck me as odd and would continue to do so until years later, when I began to spend a bit more time in Europe, and learned that cold cuts and cheese for breakfast was business as usual in a lot of places. But as I sat down for breakfast in Joan's kitchen that morning, I figured she was either bat-shit crazy or simply the kind of gal who liked to play by her own rules.

"Screw it," I imagined her thinking. "I'll serve David these cold cuts and cheese for breakfast and that bitch will *like* it."

I'd probably need to log some time with an analyst to fully understand why, but it only made me like her more for some reason.

I returned to Joan's every few months after that first visit. Slowly, we got to know each other better and became friends. It turned out we had a lot in common, quickly discovering a shared appreciation for art, vodka, *The Daily Show*, toast, and a bunch of other stuff besides those things. And, given my status at the time as either an oft-unemployed person or just plain old drifter, depending on whom you asked, I was usually able to travel on the drop of a fucking dime. So if you were looking for someone who wouldn't bother to speak up after you missed his exit and maybe even the next ten after that, I was your guy. Most of the time, though, I'd just hop a plane, train, or bus to New York and put my feet up at Joan's place for a little while.

On some of my visits, there would be another guest or two at Joan's place, usually dudes traveling alone, so I would eventually stay in almost every room in the apartment, depending on who might already be there when I rolled into town. When the bedrooms were all taken, Joan would just throw some sheets and a pillow down on a couch in the den or living room and I'd make a mental note to wear pants a bit more often. In a weird way, I felt more welcome on the couch. Somehow it felt more like I was a guest in her home rather than just some guy from Cleveland paying forty bucks a night to crash in a bedroom that would otherwise be an elaborate storage closet more than anything else.

On one such visit, I discovered, on a bookcase in her living room, an old black-and-white picture of Joan. She looked to be somewhere in her forties, dressed to kill in a black dress, sitting on a brick wall, smoking a cigarette in a way that made smoking look like the best idea ever. And, as I'd suspected, she was absolutely gorgeous, the kind of woman I probably would have run from if I happened to be passing by that brick wall just then.

"That was taken in Prague," Joan said, suddenly appearing in the doorway to catch me mid-ogle. "I lived there for a while years ago."

"Oh, cool," I said, resisting the urge to scream like she did on our first meeting. "I've always wanted to go there."

"You should," Joan told me.

"Maybe I will," I replied, playing it cool as I set the picture back down on the bookcase like it was no big deal at all.

Some time after that, I came to town for a few days, which began with my dropping my bag off at Joan's before walking out into the rain to grab some Indian food a few blocks away on Broadway. When I got to the restaurant, it was empty. Still, despite the fact that I was flying solo and there were at least a dozen smaller tables, the waiter sat me at a table for eight, something I decided to just roll with because I try to be non-confrontational with people who have access to my food. When a Finnish family of five walked in a couple minutes later, the waiter sat them at my table, too, something they also decided to just roll with. Making matters worse, the food wasn't great. So between that and the fact that I had to eat it while an entire northern European family looked on officially put that night in the loss column for me.

"They're talking about me," I thought as I struggled through some curry chicken that sure didn't taste like it. "I *know* they're talking about me."

A few days earlier, my parents, in an effort to be supportive of my black-sheep status in the family, had given me a copy of *The Artist's Way*, a book for the difficult to employ. As part of reading the book, you're supposed to keep a journal, and I had decided to become diligent about it, carrying a notebook with me everywhere and scribbling in it like a fifteen-year-old goth each morning. Naturally, I woke up early the day after my Indian restaurant debacle to tear that place a new one, something I admittedly felt kind of silly about immediately afterward, when I walked into Joan's living room and turned on the TV just in time to see United Airlines flight 175 plow into the South Tower of the World Trade Center. By this time, Joan had pretty much taken to keeping vampire hours, staying up until four or five in the morning every night before finally dragging herself to bed. So it wasn't until noon that she finally shuffled into the living room, having just woken up.

"What's happening?" she asked, her sleep mask still on her forehead.

On any other day, I would have interpreted her question as mostly rhetorical. But today was, of course, different.

"Grab a chair," I told her, cranking up the television as loud as it would go. "You've missed a couple things."

As far as the aftermath of terror attacks goes, I'd like to think we made good company for each other. But as tragic as things were in lower Manhattan and beyond, things weren't exactly great at Joan's place then, either. That past summer, Joan had taken in a long-term guest named Jim, an ex-con in his fifties who had been living at a halfway house where one of the members of her activist group worked. Apparently, the activist group member thought Joan's apartment might be a good place for Jim to get back on his proverbial feet. But somewhere along the way, things had unfortunately taken a dark turn, as evidenced in part by the heated arguments, most of which involved Jim doing all the yelling, which I'd begun hearing before either of them realized I'd walked in the door.

"He's intentionally breaking things around the apartment," Joan told me one day. "Plates, lamps, you name it."

"We were lovers briefly and, now that we're not, she wants me out," Jim told me another time. "But I hope you realize I would never hurt her."

"And I hope you realize you'd be a dead man if you ever did," I told him.

I wasn't really sure what to believe, but, given that I was definitely on Team Joan and that Jim had also once made fun of my sideburns, I fully supported her decision to move him into the tiny maid's quarters off the kitchen and to put a lock on the French doors leading to the rest of the apartment so that the bastard was no longer free to roam the place, destroying everything in his wake. I asked Joan why she didn't just send him packing altogether, but apparently Jim had contacted a housing lawyer who told him Joan was somehow legally obligated to let him stay. And, if she gave him the boot, the lawyer explained, Jim could blow the whistle on her bed-and-breakfast operation and she might lose her apartment altogether.

This latest development made my delightfully strange visits to Joan's suddenly even stranger but not nearly as delightful; as in addition to now watching Jim like a hawk, I'd have to pass through a locked door to access that plate of cold cuts and cheese slices I'd grown fond of, wolf them down, and race back to the other side of the apartment, quickly locking the door behind me before a now even more volatile Jim discovered me on his side of the French doors and tried to engage me in a bit of awkward conversation.

"Hey, Dave," he'd say, suddenly appearing in the doorway of the kitchen while fiddling with a pocketknife or doing something else that suggested he wasn't very fun. "You talk to Joan lately?"

"No, no, I haven't," I'd reply, trying to keep my focus on breakfast. "Cold cut?"

Eventually, Joan got her own housing lawyer and, shortly after, the police showed up to remove Jim from the building once and for all. Joan asked me to help with the job. To this day I'm not sure if she really felt that the police might need my help or if she was just trying to give me something to do so that I might feel somehow essential to the operation, but either way, I did my part by standing in the hallway as the cops led Jim away, ready to give him the finger if he even thought about looking in my direction.

"I love you," Marjorie, a sixtysomething woman staying in one of the other guest rooms that week—whom, it's also worth noting, I'd just met—told me afterward.

"Dammit," I thought. "Just when it seemed like things were getting back to normal around here."

Still, sometimes it's best to just tell people what they want to hear, so I told Marjorie I loved her, too, and made a mental note to keep the door to my room locked for at least the rest of the day.

My visits to Joan's continued for the next year or so, until I finally ended up coming to New York for good in early 2003 and figured if there was going to be some creep staying in her maid's quarters, then it might as well be me. With that in mind, Joan let me move in until I found my own place a couple months later, almost immediately after which she was diagnosed with breast cancer. By then, I was one of the few constant characters in her life, so we both decided I'd probably make as good a nurse as any during her recovery period.

On the day of her release, I picked Joan up from the hospital and took her home, where an old friend of hers, Father Daniel Berrigan, the famed activist and poet,* joined us for some cele-bratory vodka in the living room. Father Berrigan had been a member of her activist group, which by now had stopped meeting at her place.

"Do you ever get involved in protests?" he asked me at one point.

---

* As an example, in 1967, Daniel and his brother, the Josephite priest Philip Berrigan, were arrested for pouring blood on draft records as part of the Bal-timore Four, a group protesting the Vietnam War among other things. In 1968, he whipped up some homemade napalm and, with eight other Catholic protesters, used it to destroy 378 draft files in Catonsville, Maryland. In short, Daniel Berrigan doesn't just talk the talk, he walks the walk. Think about that next time you're tackling the tough issues on Facebook and calling it a day.

"My whole life is a protest," I told him. "Refill?"

"Sure," he said, holding his glass out.

The homecoming party out of the way, it was now time for the dirty work. Joan had had a mastectomy, so she'd need special care after her surgery that would involve, among other things, draining a mixture of blood, pus, and whatever else through small tubes protruding from her chest twice a day. The tubes would have to be gradually and methodically "milked" before I could empty their contents into a clear plastic container and dispose of them in the bathroom while doing my best to act like I did stuff like this all the time. On one level it was pretty gross, but on another it was kind of nice because I knew if I could do that sort of thing with a smile, most other stuff in life would be a walk in the park. Plus, it took a good ten or fifteen minutes each time, and gave Joan and me a chance to catch up.

"Did you see *The Daily Show* the other night?" she'd ask.

"Yup," I'd say. "I caught the end of it."

"That Jon Stewart is so funny," she'd say. "And handsome."

"I'll say," I'd reply. "I mean I think he's funny, too—the handsome part I can't comment on either way because that sort of thing honestly doesn't even register with me since I'm so straight."

"Right, David," Joan would say. "Of course."

Afterward, I'd head into the kitchen to whip up some dinner for the two of us.

"I really like how everything is kind of charred," Joan would say politely as she picked little bits of blackened food from her teeth. "It gives things a sort of crunchy texture one might not expect from chicken with vegetables."

It was the best.

My nursing duties lasted a few weeks, after which I went back to staying in the tiny room I was renting at the Chelsea Hotel at the time. And while Joan seemed to make at least a partial recovery from her breast cancer, she always played it pretty close to the vest when it came to giving me health updates, so I never knew for sure what was really going on. As best I could tell, though, the cancer remained an ongoing concern and, given that she was now in her eighties and had decided to skip further treatment, would probably catch up with her sooner rather than later.

We stayed in regular contact, by afternoon visits to her place or phone calls that would usually entail my shouting into the phone for a few minutes before she told me she needed to go lie down.

"I already know what I'm gonna do when I'm gone," Joan told me one day over tea. "I'm going to be stardust just flying around New York City with the birds."

I'd never heard someone speak of their post-death plans with such a mixture of nonchalance and certainty. There was something nice about it. This way I wouldn't have to wonder; I could just take Joan at her word.

"Just promise me you won't fall in with the wrong crowd of pigeons or anything," I told her.

"I promise, David," she said.

In the last year or so before her death, Joan began to receive regular visits from a nurse who didn't drink so much on the job. And to make sure she had someone nearby around the clock, Joan's daughter, Connie, moved in with her, too. Connie was in her fifties and usually wore thick turtleneck sweaters and long gray braids that suggested if you felt like, say, listening to Grateful Dead bootlegs 24/7 or maybe talking about how delicious kale is even though everyone knows it isn't, she wasn't exactly going to fight you on that. And while I never set foot in her room, I'd bet my pancreas it was crystals, dreamcatchers, and majestic wolf posters as far as the eye could see. Anyway, whenever I'd stop by Joan's after that, she'd usually distract Connie with something in the kitchen before we went to hang out together somewhere else in the apartment.

"That book on Wicca you ordered came in the mail today," Joan might tell her. "I left it on the counter next to the tea bags."

"Oh, good!" she'd reply before slipping on a pair of John Lennon reading glasses and digging in at least until I left.

On what ended up being my last visit with Joan, she and I sat for a while in her den, where she'd recently been staying busy filling massive binders with old pictures and letters. She could still get up and around and had a bit of energy left, but, to use Joan's words, her stardust days weren't far off. With this in mind, she had begun gradually assembling these binders, one for each decade of her life.

"This one is from when I was in my forties," Joan said, opening a binder onto the coffee table to reveal a couple more pictures of her laughing and smoking on that brick wall in Prague. For a second, I imagined some lucky guy on the other side of the camera, snapping away as he laughed and smoked along with her, before I flipped ahead a few pages to find snapshots of Joan smiling at dinner with friends, sitting in some living room with presumably long-gone relatives, or just standing there all alone, posing elegantly for the camera. Mixed in with the pictures were cards, letters, and the occasional page or two from an old diary. Some of the notes were sunny, expressing thanks or wishing a happy something or other. Others were less so, alluding to some soured romance or a relative she'd rather not run into in that living room again.

As I finished perusing the first binder, Joan pushed another one toward me.

"This one is from when I was in my thirties," she said, "back when I was living in Chicago."

I opened that one to, of course, find photos of a younger Joan, still having dinner with friends and hanging out with relatives and all that, but also dancing, usually in elaborate outfits involving bare midriffs and other details that had me suddenly paying closer attention and turning the pages much more slowly. Sure, Joan had told me before that she had been a dancer, but not a smoking-hot one who appeared to be roughly my age at the time. And as I sat there next to her several decades later, doing my damnedest to keep my eyeballs from leaving my skull, I began to wonder, "Is it inappropriate for me to be sitting here with my dear friend Joan, now in the winter of her life, as I get all worked up over photos of her from back in her younger days?"

I felt ashamed for a moment before suddenly flipping the binder shut and leaning back against the couch to catch a quick breath.

"Thanks for sharing these with me, Joan," I told her. "It really means a lot."

"I'm glad you enjoyed them," she said, and smiled.

"Yeah," I said. "Now, where's the binder from when you were in your twenties?"

QUALITY TIME

ONE OF THE GREAT THINGS ABOUT HAVING A WHOLE house for you and your dad to hang out in together is you can both just disappear into separate rooms on opposite sides of the place for hours and hours at a time pretty much whenever you feel like it, sometimes even in mid-conversation.

"They put in a new section at the grocery dedicated entirely to cheese, you know," my dad might say to me.

"That's really great," I'd reply. "Because I like cheese."

"Well, then you're definitely going to want to check out this new cheese section," he'd say. "They've got it all: mild cheddar, sharp cheddar, Swiss cheese, goat cheese, Monterey Jack, some of the other ones, brie, Camembert . . ."

By the time he got through listing the majority of the cheeses out there today, I'd be long gone.

In recent months, my dad had become really busy with his

"paperwork," a dizzying tapestry of various financial statements, insurance forms, notes only he could possibly read, and whatever else might have been swept up into the mix during normal business hours, now covering most flat surfaces in the kitchen. He'd try to explain it all to me from time to time, but there were never enough pictures to hold my interest and I'd usually wind up with a headache before he could finish.

"But I don't understand," I'd say to him. "If I didn't *intentionally* cause the toilet to overflow, then wouldn't that technically be considered an 'act of God,' too?"

"Let's just start from the beginning," he'd reply.

Anyway, while he'd usually stay busy with that stuff during the time we were apart yet still under the same roof, I'd usually wander upstairs to lie down for a while in what was once my bedroom but was now known as the "guest room," reserved for any and all visitors who weren't me. Sometimes I'd just stare at the ceiling, trying to find faces or hidden messages in the stucco. Other times I'd stare out the window at views that, aside from the trees now being either much taller or chopped down altogether, remained mostly unchanged from when I was a kid. It was comforting that way—I could just be a kid again for a little while, a kid in some strange yet familiar room that my parents had painted mustard yellow and installed ACE bandage–beige carpeting in after they had foolishly convinced themselves there was no chance I'd ever be back in there staring at the ceiling for hours on end.

"David, this is the guest room," my mom used to say to me when she'd catch me in there. "Get out."

It was at this point that I'd usually wander back downstairs to the Barcalounger to see what kind of crazy shit Angela and Tony were getting up to on back-to-back reruns of *Who's the Boss?*, which somehow seemed to be on nearly every time I turned on the TV, not that I'm complaining the least bit. Somehow the sound of Judith Light's voice gave me solace, even when the 100 percent understandable sexual tension between her and Tony Danza as he completed ordinary house chores right in front of her pushed her to the brink. Most of the time, I didn't really even watch—I simply made use of the Barcalounger's convenient reclining feature, closed my eyes, and soaked it all in, confident in the knowledge that, at least for the next half hour or so, everything was going to be mostly okay.

But wherever I might disappear to during my visits home to see my dad, eventually we'd regroup in the kitchen to try and figure out what to do about dinner.

"Wanna go to Rigoletto's?" I asked, referring to the Italian place up the street.

"Sure," he said. "Just let me use the restroom real quick."

By now I was well aware that "real quick" usually meant that I could probably squeeze in a nap or maybe even complete an elaborate jigsaw puzzle before we left. You'd think my dad might emerge with hair worthy of James Brown in his prime in that time, but it was somehow never the case. Regardless, about forty-five minutes later, we made the short drive to Rigoletto's, walked in, and requested a table for two. Rigoletto's is your typical neighborhood Italian place: a mural of someplace Italian looking on one wall, some photos of pizza on another, and red vinyl upholstery as far as the eye can see. We'd been coming here since I was a kid, and it seemed like all the same waitresses from back then were still working there, too. Sometimes I thought they might hate me, other times I was sure of it. But the place was at least consistent, so it was always nice to come back.

"Should we get pizza?" my dad asked after we settled into a booth.

"Yes," I answered. "And spaghetti."

"We can't get pizza and spaghetti," my dad said, thus starting the same argument we've been having since the eighties.

"Why not?" I asked.

"Because I said so," he replied.

"But I want pizza and spaghetti," I told him.

"Well, you can't have it," he said.

"Yes, I can," I countered. "Because I'm an adult."

He just shook his head after that, like his neck was hurting or something.

When the waitress finally came back around and dropped off our Cokes in the same red plastic cups almost every pizza place in Cleveland seems to be required by law to use, we ordered a large pizza with pepperoni, sausage, onions, and mushrooms. I could tell my dad felt like he'd scored some sort of victory over me as I watched our waitress shuffle away with her notepad, but what he didn't realize was that when I told him I had to use the restroom immediately afterward, I was really going to hunt down that waitress and tell her to put in an order of spaghetti while she was at it.

"What do you have going on the rest of the week?" my dad asked as I returned to our booth.

"Not much," I said.

"What about next week?" he asked.

"Next week is shaping up to be not much so far, too," I told him.

"Shouldn't you be finding stuff to do?" he asked.

"I figured I should keep myself available in case you needed my help with anything," I explained.

"Like what?" he asked.

"Anything," I said.

"I don't really need help with anything."

"Maybe not now. But when you do, I'll be there. Waiting."

I could tell this conversation was headed nowhere fast, so I was relieved when the waitress showed up with our spaghetti in near-record time. I was starving, but even better than finally being able to eat was the look on my dad's face when he saw that spaghetti.

"Want some?" I asked him, holding up the giant serving spoon the waitress had thrown at my head upon delivery. I knew if he said yes, then my dad couldn't say a damn thing about my sneaking off to order spaghetti. And as he reached for his fork with a slight scowl, I knew I had won this round.

After we finished stuffing our faces for a solid twenty minutes, I apologized to my dad for forgetting my wallet, thanked him for paying for dinner, and we headed back outside to the Buick.

"I told you we ordered too much," he said, nodding at the doggie bag full of leftover pizza and spaghetti tucked under his arm.

"No, we didn't," I corrected him.

"Then what are all these leftovers?" he countered.

"Those are for later," I explained. "Now can I please have the car keys?"

"Why?" he asked.

"So I can drive home," I told him.

"But I want to drive home," he said.

"How are you gonna drive *and* hold all those leftovers?" I asked him.

It wasn't a very solid argument, but my dad threw me the car keys anyway before sliding into the passenger seat.

"Is it hard being a dad?" I asked as I turned the ignition.

"Yes," my dad said, pulling on his seat belt. "And it gets harder and harder every day."

"I'll bet," I told him.

We pulled into the driveway a few minutes later. Then we headed inside and my dad opened the fridge to find room for the leftovers.

"That's the weird thing about pizza and spaghetti," I said to him.

"What is?" he asked.

"Well, pizza you have to pretty much eat by the next day or you're screwed—the crust gets too hard," I told him. "But see, with spaghetti, you can have a little bit the next day, put the rest back in the fridge, pull it out again the next day, have some more, put the rest back in the fridge, maybe have a little more the day after that, and on and on for the rest of the week usually and it's great every time. You don't even have to heat it up first if you don't want. You don't even have to move from in front of the refrigerator."

I had hoped to hear his thoughts on all that, but before I even finished, he had already gone upstairs to bed for some reason. I still had a little fire left in me, though, so I walked into the family room, settled into the Barcalounger, and turned on the TV to find Angela and Tony, together in the kitchen again, just trying to make sense of it all.

A MEETING
OF THE MINDS

THE YEAR WAS 2004. BOTH NBC'S *THE APPRENTICE* and really fun cell-phone ringtones had taken an unsuspecting public by storm. I had managed to elude both—I kept my phone on vibrate and was ready to stare in bemusement at anyone even thinking of telling me I had been "fired."

But I needed money, so when the call came to write ringtones for Donald Trump, a quiet businessman from Queens who had been reluctantly thrust into the spotlight by the seventh-most popular program on network television at the time, I said yes. I had been doing some freelance writing and one of my clients was among the tangle of corporations assigned to the case. Fortunately, they decided to throw me a bone.

Of course, I knew a thing or two about Trump already. He had flawless hair; he slept on piles of money each night; given the choice between having something not gold-plated or entirely gold-plated, he chose door number two every time. Still, I wanted to do the best job possible, so I had one of Trump's minions send me copies of two of his books, *Trump: The Art of the Deal** and *Trump: The Art of the Comeback,* as well as an anatomically correct Trump doll that would tell me all sorts of things every time I pressed its back, something I couldn't help but do repeatedly as soon as it came into my possession.

"You really think you're a good leader?" the doll would ask, seemingly out of the blue. "I don't."

A little harsh, maybe, but also something I probably needed to hear.

Despite all the hours I spent playing with that doll, though, I had my work cut out for me. Somehow, in what I can only assume was the result of someone putting a gun to Trump's head, NBC owned the rights to his electrifying catchphrase "You're fired!" The challenge was mine to figure out what else he might say—to write some slogans people might want to hear coming out of their phones besides those two magical words that had already galvanized a nation.

"Your services are no longer required at this place of business!"

"Please stop showing up here for work, okay?"

"Die, you anus!"

These are but a few of the alternatives to "You're fired!" that I proposed. In the end, though, it was decided that Trump's ringtone avatar would be less cutthroat and more inspirational, encouraging cell-phone users to answer promptly so they could take

---

* It's worth nothing that Donald Trump himself has called this book his second favorite of all time, the first, of course, being the Bible. And while I'll admit both have their moments, it's important to remember not to interpret either of them literally.

advantage of a big business opportunity or maybe just hurt some-one's feelings. I whipped up a few dozen Trumpist gems. Track 'em down if you like; I imagine they're still out there somewhere, priced to move.

"This is Donald Trump. I have no choice but to tell you . . . you're getting a phone call."

"I'm Donald Trump and this is the call of a lifetime!"

"This is Donald Trump. Answer your phone now—it might be me calling."

Maybe not my finest hour, but, hey—the customer is always right. After that, I assumed my work was done, but I ended up being asked to attend the actual taping, too, at none other than Trump Tower.

"You mean I'll actually be in the room while Donald is saying the stuff I wrote?" I asked a guy from the ringtone concern.

"Yes," he said, placing a hand on my shoulder for emphasis.

This was officially about to be the biggest thing anyone in my family had ever done, including fighting in wars or any of that other crap my older relatives always went on about. Naturally, I couldn't wait to tell them.

"I'm working with Donald Trump," I told my mom over the phone.

"Who?" my mom asked.

"Donald Trump," I told her. "The guy from *The Apprentice*."

"David got a job with Tony Crump," my mom yelled to my dad in the next room.

"That's nice," my dad yelled back.

They were pumped.

When the big day rolled around, I put on a suit and tie and

worked as many hair products into my scalp as possible before heading over to Trump's offices in midtown Manhattan to meet the other dozen or so people required to complete a task of this magnitude.

As expected, Trump HQ was beyond opulent. It was as if a blind decorator had been given an unlimited budget and told he'd never work in this town again.

"This way, please," a Trump representative, who was difficult to focus on amid all that sparkle, said before leading us to a conference room. Along the way, I spotted Donald Jr. sitting in an adjacent office, his hair perfect, as he no doubt bought or sold something or maybe even someone without even thinking about it. It ruled.

"You have one hour," the rep announced, prompting everyone in the conference room to spring into action, turning it into a makeshift recording studio. A few minutes later, the doors opened and in walked Trump, somehow looking even Trumpier than I'd anticipated. He wore a suit and tie and, of course, his trademark scowl. And though he stood mere feet from me, I found I had no further insight into his hair-care regimen. Looking into his coiffure did nothing to demystify it. In fact, it only confused me more.

"Right this way, Mr. Trump," a ringtone specialist said, gently urging him toward the microphones while being careful not to actually touch him.

"Let's make this quick," Trump grunted, already sounding like the ringtones I'd written. "I've got a busy day ahead of me."

At this point, a mild panic set in as everyone in the room became convinced he or she might very well be "fired" or at least told to wait by the elevators at any moment. As for me, though,

I couldn't help but relax a bit; it had suddenly occurred to me that Trump might not be the oblivious blowhard everyone thinks. I mean, sure, he was a blowhard, maybe even the biggest blowhard of all time, but he also seemed totally self-aware, like he knew he was just playing a character, and that as soon as we left, he'd run into Ivanka's office, shut the door behind him, and squeal, "I got 'em again, honey!" Something about that made me actually kind of like the guy, if I sat there and thought about it long enough.

Moments later, after a technician had scrambled to hit any and all record buttons, Trump began barreling through the ringtones, printed on large cue cards that would remain easily readable even when he squinted judgmentally, which was always. Occasionally he'd give emphasis to a different word or see if getting angrier might help sell things a bit more. Meanwhile, everyone else in the room remained pinned to the wall, just trying to get through the proceedings intact.

Things seemed to be going well enough until about twenty minutes later, when Trump paused abruptly and began scanning the room in the manner that, by now, haunts people's dreams the world over.

"Who wrote these things?" he barked, pointing at the cue cards like he wanted them taken out back and shot.

"That guy! Dave Hill!" at least five people volunteered in unison, their tone suggesting they would happily stab me right then and there if Trump would just say the word.

I figured I might start gathering my things at this point, but before I could, Trump looked at me, dropped his scowl, and said, "You're a very good writer."

"Thanks," I said with a nod, sensing a trap. For the remaining forty minutes or so of the recording session, Trump refused to address anyone in the room but me. Others tried to intervene, but as soon as they finished talking, Trump would turn to me, his right-hand man, and ask, "What do you think, Dave?"

It was a weird kind of trust to have earned, sure, but it was also kind of cool—especially considering that otherwise I probably would have been just sitting at home scanning Craigslist for missed connections.

As the session wrapped up, I recalled something else I'd learned about Trump through my tireless research: he hates shaking hands. Naturally, this made my mission clear. This will be the true test of our love, I thought as I stood waiting for any others brazen enough to approach Trump to say whatever they were gonna say with their hands glued to their sides before getting the hell out of his sight, dammit.

With the path clear, I approached him for some bro time.

"Nice working with you, Donald," I told him.

"You, too, Dave," he said.

"Thanks," I replied. I gingerly extended my hand. I could feel eyebrows across the room rising in slow-motion panic.

Will he? Won't he?

Against all odds, Trump slowly reached out and grabbed my hand, shaking it not so firmly, as if to suggest his henchmen might be waiting for me outside and not so softly as if to suggest a quality hang in Montauk was off the table. No, this was just right—perfect, in fact, almost like he was a regular human being who had done this sort of thing before. All these years later, that shake still feels like a victory of some sort, but I'm not sure for whom.

As I sit here writing this in my underpants, Donald Trump continues his disturbing bid for the American presidency. And I find myself hoping more than ever that he really is only playing a character, that maybe he's just the greatest performance artist of our time, a modern-day Warhol or slightly chattier Marina Abramović* who will any day now say "Tada!" and take a bow, then go open an all-you-can-eat shrimp joint in the Outer Banks or something.

With each passing day, I fear I may be wrong. Still, whatever happens, it'll always be nice to look back on that day at Trump Tower and think, "Sure, he's a hate-spewing boob who somehow manages to sound even angrier and crazier than that doll I still can't help but drag out from under the bed every once in a while . . . and, yes, he's even got that certain awful something to win the endorsement of the unicellular Sarah Palin. But put the two of us in a room together for an hour and, goddamn, do that son of a bitch and I make one hell of a ringtone."

---

* Please note that the fact that I have now mentioned Marina Abramović *twice* in this book is something I never saw coming, either.

THE JOY OF COOKING

I WAS READING SOMETHING ON THE INTERNET THE other day about multitasking and how it's basically the worst and will one day kill us all.* Apparently, as we go about simultaneously responding to e-mails, taking a hard stance on something really important on Facebook, tweeting something seriously retweetable, texting someone who's been waiting like nine minutes or something for a reply, and whatever else could possibly be left after that, our brains reward us by releasing chemicals that fool us into thinking that we are really tearing our day a new one and kicking ass at every turn. In reality, however, as researchers holed up in some research building far, far away are finding, all this multitasking is getting us next to nowhere and it's actually

---

* Okay, they didn't actually mention the thing about killing, but they did say it was bad, and I know how to read between the lines, thank you.

much more effective to just do one thing at a time, like our ancestors, with their crazy beards, high-waisted pants, and penchant for goggles, did so many years ago.

Of course, some—millennials and climate-change deniers, for example—will try to blame multitasking on the futuristic times* in which we live. But, according to my research, it's been going on since the seventies at least, which is coincidentally when I first began to notice it. The biggest offender, as best I could tell, was my mother, who I don't think did it for that chemical reward I was talking about earlier, but because with a husband, five kids, a full-time job, and the occasional house pet all vying for her attention, she simply had no choice. Usually she managed to juggle things pretty well. And when she didn't, sometimes it worked out for the best anyway, like the time she accidentally popped a Klonopin instead of an aspirin while preparing Thanksgiving dinner back in the nineties. It might have been the first time I ever saw her sit back, relax, and really enjoy the holiday. And the fact that she realized her error halfway through a second glass of wine only helped matters.

"It's nice to see you joining us at the table for a change instead of frantically running back and forth between the dining room and the kitchen all night," my sister Libby remarked.

"Maybe *you're* having a t-table," my mom replied. "What's your favorite candy?"

To this day it remains one of my fondest family memories.

---

* Speaking of which, where are the silver onesies and four-course meals in pill form they promised us? This is bullshit. I'm tired of being lied to.

. . .

But things weren't always perfect.

My four siblings and I were all born within a five-and-a-half-year age range, so the race to survive was usually pretty tight during our childhood. And, given her busy schedule and on-the-go lifestyle and all, mealtimes often involved my mother just throwing a large shank of meat and maybe a microwaved potato or two on the table and quickly jumping out of the way before my siblings and I attacked. Usually everyone would get enough. And if they didn't, they could just make up for it with an extra bowl or two of breakfast cereal, which we kept in a closet with all our coats and shoes next to the side door. I'm still not sure why we kept the cereal in the closet like that, and even all these years later it seems best not to question it. The important thing to remember is that my brother, Bob, survived almost entirely on stale and just-the-right-amount-of-mildew raisin bran for at least half the eighties.

Anyway, one Saturday when I was about seven, my mother followed a long day of house chores and seemingly random scolding by whipping up a big steak for the family. It maybe wasn't the choicest cut, so before throwing it in the oven she decided to marinate it for a while, making it easier for our prepubescent hands to tear the meat off the bone at feeding time.

It was the weekend, we were all moving at a more leisurely pace, and it turned out to be one of those rare occasions when all of us, with the exception of my sister Libby, who was away at summer camp somewhere in Colorado, were able to take the time to sit down at the table for dinner that evening.

"Make sure everyone gets some," my mom said, setting a Pyrex dish containing the still-sizzling discount meat in the center of the kitchen table. My dad, the only one at the table with large-knife privileges, handled the cutting and distribution.

Once the meat was doled out, we all began gnawing away. It was usually at this point that things would go quiet for at least a couple of minutes while we all stuffed our faces, but not tonight.

"This steak tastes funny," my oldest sister, Miriam, muttered after her first bite.

Since most reviews of the food at our home started this way, my mom didn't think much of it.

"Oh, go on," she said dismissively. "It tastes fine."

"No, Miriam's right," my brother, Bob, agreed, wrinkling his nose. "It's pretty gross."

"It's not pretty gross," my mom, growing slightly irritated, replied. "I just bought it this morning at the grocery store."

"I can't eat it," my sister Katy said, feigning dizziness while spitting a piece of half-chewed beef onto her plate, which in turn caused a disgusting-yet-probably-adorable-in-its-own-way chain reaction involving the rest of us kids doing the same.

Like most mothers, my mom was used to random and largely unwarranted complaints and even occasional food spitting from her children. But after a long day of cleaning up after all of us, she just wasn't having it.

"The steak is perfectly fine!" my mom snapped. "You know how many kids in the world would kill to be able to have a steak like this for dinner?"

"Well, give it to them, then," I told her.

Moments after I pretty much nailed it with my standard response to whenever other children in the world, starving or otherwise, were brought up at mealtimes to illustrate how ungrateful my siblings and I were, my dad got around to trying a bite of steak for himself. As he dug in, a troubled look spread across his face.

"What's wrong, Bob?" my mom asked. "Don't tell me you don't like the steak, either!"

"Well, it *does* actually taste kind of funny," my dad said, squinting ever so slightly, "kind of like Murphy's Oil Soap, in fact."

Suddenly the look on my mom's face turned from annoyed to concerned. Murphy's Oil Soap was an all-purpose cleanser she used by the gallon to clean almost everything, inorganic and sometimes otherwise, in our house, especially the kitchen. And as she quickly began to retrace her steps, my mom spun around in horror to discover an empty bottle of Murphy's Oil Soap sitting on the kitchen counter right next to an unopened container of the vegetable oil she usually used to marinate stuff that had been priced to move. It was like something out of *The Shining*.

"Oh, no!" she exclaimed, suddenly realizing what she had done. "I was talking on the phone while I was marinating the steak, and I think I accidentally poured a bottle of Murphy's Oil Soap onto the steak instead of the vegetable oil!"

As the story broke, my siblings and I began to scream and my mom began to frantically clear the tainted meat from the table.

"I poisoned everyone!" she screamed, tossing the evidence into the kitchen sink.

"Are we gonna die?" my little sister Katy screeched, voicing a concern shared by, well, me at least.

"No," my dad assured her, trying to restore some semblance of order. "Not yet."

"I'm calling the poison control hotline," my mom yelled, now officially freaking out.

Fortunately, it was the late seventies, a popular time for accidental poisonings, and we had a sticker with the poison control hotline posted right next to the phone for just such an occasion.

"Cool!" I thought.

I remembered when the sticker had come in the mail a few months earlier and, despite the circumstances, was excited to see it finally called to action as my mother dialed the number in a panic.

"I poisoned my family!" she shrieked into the phone after a few seconds.

We all watched and listened attentively as the seemingly high-stakes* conversation began to play out.

"No, I didn't do it on purpose!" my mom clarified, sounding more than a bit defensive.

It was at this point when I imagined the person on the other end pressing a record button before gesturing to a coworker to silently listen in on another receiver. At the same time, yet another coworker would place a call to the local police precinct, where just then a grizzled officer, finally set to retire and start collecting his pension after thirty long years on the force, was

---

* Or should I say "high-steaks"? (Sorry.)

informed that he better call the missus and tell her he won't be coming home tonight, after all.

Meanwhile, back in our kitchen, things continued to heat up.

"I accidentally marinated a steak in Murphy's Oil Soap and served it to my family," my mother sobbed into the receiver after a few more seconds while looking over at all of us seated at the kitchen table, presumably to etch one last memory into her brain of what we looked like when we were still alive so she could have something to think about whenever things got slow in prison.

The silence that followed as my mom listened to the person from the poison control hotline on the other end seemed to last at least long enough for me to consider maybe telling everyone in the room what I always liked about them. It was also hard not to think at least momentarily of Libby, hundreds of miles away from the scene of the crime at summer camp. "Who would break the news to her?" I wondered. Would a camp counselor quietly slip her a note during archery explaining that her mother had poisoned the rest of her family and that—should she need counseling of any sort on top of the already scheduled camp activities—it would be made available to her at no additional cost to her or her remaining loved ones? Or would she simply stumble across it on the news one night before lights-out and be forced to piece things together on her own from there?

Meanwhile, back in our kitchen, things continued to heat up even more.

"Murphy's Oil Soap," my mom repeated after the interminable pause. "I clean the house with it."

Another long silence.

"Ohhh, great," my mom then said, suddenly sounding relieved. "And yes, you're right—it *is* good for cleaning just about anything."

I could tell my mother, now almost smiling, was officially wrapping up the call.

"Okay, thank you," she said, hanging up the phone. "You have a nice night, too."

"What'd they say?" my dad, the official representative of us victims, asked.

"They said Murphy's Oil Soap is made of all-natural ingredients and there's no danger at all of anyone being poisoned by it," my mom said with a sigh. Then she walked over to the sink, turned the faucet on, and began to rinse the disgraced victuals.

"What are you doing?" I asked her.

"Rinsing the soap off the steak so you kids can eat it," she explained.

"We can't eat steak that's been covered in Murphy's Oil Soap!" Miriam protested.

"But I just told you," my mom, starting to get irritated again, replied, "the lady from the poison control hotline said it's not poisonous at all."

"It doesn't mean it's not gross," Bob said.

"You don't know what you're talking about," my mom countered while biting into the freshly rinsed flesh for emphasis. "You can barely taste the soap at all anymore! I kind of like it this way, actually—gives it a nice tang."

"We're not eating it," Miriam said, speaking for all of us.

"Yes, you are!" my mom said sternly before slapping the steak back into the newly rinsed Pyrex dish and tossing it back down in the center of the table with a clang.

"They don't have to eat the steak, Bunny," my dad finally ruled. "Let's just figure something else out for dinner tonight."

My mother stood silently for a moment, glaring at my dad, then at us kids, and then back at my dad again.

"Fine, but these goddamn assy kids are spoiled!"* my mom barked, grabbing the Pyrex dish from the table and reluctantly tossing the sudsy steak into the garbage. "And I'm damn sick of it, too—that was a perfectly good steak!"

Then she stormed out of the kitchen, disappearing for a few minutes before begrudgingly meeting us all out in the driveway so my dad could take us to McDonald's, where we were allowed to order whatever we wanted within reason. All things considered, except for the part where my short life flashed before my eyes, it turned out to be a pretty fun night. Still, all these years later, I sometimes wonder how my mom got so distracted that she actually mistook a bottle of cleanser for a bottle of vegetable oil. But even more than that, I wonder how it never occurred to any of us to ask my dad how in the hell he knew what Murphy's Oil Soap tasted like in the first place.

---

* "Goddamn assy kids" was what my mother, who somehow never seemed able to grasp the proper mechanics of profanity or any sort of rude talk in general, called us when she'd been pushed to her limit. It was the best, and I really miss it.

CLEVELAND NOIR

IT WAS A COLD, DAMP NIGHT IN CLEVELAND, WHICH IS to say pretty much just like most other nights in Cleveland, as I slipped my dad's Buick into neutral and quietly rolled out the driveway and into the sexy, suburban night. It was just my dad and I in the house now, and he kept his ears sharp.

I was careful to leave the headlights off until I was at least halfway down the block so there would be little chance I'd be forced to pull over and listen to all the usual claptrap about how it was "his car" and he "might need it later" from my dad, the cops, or anyone else looking to cock-block my freedom. I instinctively pointed the car in the direction of downtown, as I was looking for trouble, the good kind, the kind that guys like me get into without even really trying. First, I dipped down into Cleveland Heights, wending my way through blocks upon blocks of sleepy single-family homes, their living rooms aglow in the pale-blue light of basic cable, and then past St. Ann's, the rival elementary school of my youth, where at least a dozen fifth-graders once stopped cold in the middle of recess to give me the finger in unison for reasons I still struggle to understand as I type this. From there I spun into slightly less glamorous East Cleveland, where boarded-up storefronts, bars, and restaurants covered in graffiti and the occasional crudely rendered penis drawing* mocked my thirst for action and shards of broken glass littered the sidewalks, glistening in the night like bogus diamonds begging to be discovered and hastily scooped up with bare hands before finally you realize, "Dammit—it's just glass and—help!—I'm bleeding."

Minutes later, I barreled into Cleveland proper, where streetlamps threatening to go on the blink at any minute bathed the urban landscape in a sepia not unlike the color of the stale urine of some sad sack who should probably get that checked. And fast. As best I could tell, it was a slow night, even for Cleveland—a guy waiting for the bus on one corner, another guy waiting for seemingly nothing at all on another, but not a whole lot else in terms of what might qualify as guaranteed excitement.

I pressed on across the Lorain-Carnegie Bridge, which—as is hinted at in the name—connects Lorain Avenue to Carnegie Avenue and also crosses over the Cuyahoga River.† When I was in

---

* I don't know what it is about penis drawings, but as best I can tell, if you leave a wall of any sort unattended long enough, someone will eventually come along and draw a penis on that thing. And not long after that, someone else is sure to come along and draw a smiley face on that penis. I don't support this kind of behavior in most instances (it really depends on the wall), but I will say it's one of the few things you can really count on in life.

† In case you were wondering, contrary to popular belief, the Cuyahoga River isn't even slightly on fire and hasn't been for about forty years now, so everyone just needs to shut up about it already. Geez.

high school, some unruly bastard tossed a bottle off the bridge and hit Mötley Crüe drummer Tommy Lee's then-wife, Heather Locklear, square in the forehead while the two shared a romantic and—one hopes—intercourse-filled ferryboat ride down the Cuyahoga. I felt bad for Heather; but then, as now, the incident served to remind me that Cleveland is a magical place where anything is possible, where if you really set your mind to it there is almost nothing you can't achieve, where one minute you're just some poor schlub on some slowly crumbling bridge, giving local open-container laws the finger, and the next you're a sharp-shooter sending the star of *T. J. Hooker* straight to the emergency room, like it was your job. As my wheels hit the potholed concrete of Lorain Avenue and the mouth of historic yet occasionally seedy Ohio City at the end of the bridge, I acknowledged to myself that I'd be one happy young man if tonight shaped up to be even half as life affirming.

A flew blocks into things, I already noticed that Ohio City was well on its way to leaving downtown Cleveland in the dust, in terms of real action. To wit, I counted at least five people waiting for the bus and at least two different women in tight pants, peddling their flesh or possibly just running errands or—who knows?—maybe even both as they shambled down the sidewalk, making furtive glances at passing cars and sucking on cigarettes like they were in a smoking contest or something. My mood was hopeful as I continued down the avenue past Saint Ignatius High School, my alma mater, where on at least one occasion I earned second honors, even though I totally could have gotten first honors if I felt like it.

"Suckers," I thought as I spotted two acne-riddled students

with loosened ties and backpacks slung over their shoulders am-
bling toward the school parking lot, presumably after finishing
up some marathon after-school activity for nerds or something.

Twenty fast blocks later, I passed the Hot Dog Inn, which,
despite its promising name, is not a hot dog–themed hotel at all
but merely a restaurant that specializes in hot dogs best consumed while drunk to the point of medical concern. I thought
to stop in before remembering that it was in almost this exact
same spot years before that some nut job threw an empty liquor
bottle at my mom's station wagon, shattering it instantly against
the backseat passenger window in what I can only assume was a
failed bid to take down the king.*

"Heather and I—we're not so different, after all," I thought
before rolling up the car window and applying my foot to the gas
pedal a touch harder in the event that my would-be assailant was
waiting in the wings with a fresh bottle, renewed determination,
and at least slightly improved aim.

A few blocks later, I spotted a nondescript bar that as best
I could tell went by the name of just "bar." There was an old
Harley-Davidson panhead motorcycle parked out front, which I
took to be a harbinger of both kindred spirits and instant good
times awaiting me inside, so I decided to bang a left onto the
nearest side street, give the Buick a rest, and see what was
what.

Moments after checking and rechecking that I'd locked my
dad's car with the electronic clicker thing that made the horn go
off enough times that at least one neighborhood resident felt the

---

* I.e., me.

need to shoot me a dirty look through his blinds, I flung the door of the bar open to discover a wood-paneled room with no one inside except for a potbellied bartender and a curly-haired fireplug of a woman of about fifty or so whom I decided to hold responsible for the fact that Wilson Phillips was playing on the jukebox. I say this not to suggest that I have any beef with Wilson Phillips—I don't, not even a little bit. In fact, as far as musical groups featuring the children of members of both the Beach Boys and the Mamas and the Papas go, they are as good as it gets, if you ask me.

After a quick spin around the room to fully appreciate the wretchedness of the place, I took a seat at the corner of the bar and gave the bartender the usual nod I use in these situations, the kind that says, "I see you, and it is my sense that you work here." He had tanned, leathery skin and long, graying hair worn in a ratty, half-assed ponytail, but the resentful yet youthful glint in his eyes suggested his weathered look was more about miles than years and he, in fact, probably wasn't that much older than I. The bartender's brow was knitted in frustration as he fidgeted with a wristwatch, one of those old silver ones with the expanding band that pulls annoyingly at your arm hairs until you finally decide you don't really give a crap what time it is anyway and throw it in the trash. Since my nod didn't succeed in pulling his focus one bit, I decided to try a little conversation.

"Watch trouble, huh?" I asked.

"It's broke," he said, not even slightly looking up.

"You mean it's only right twice a day?" I said, following up with what I still consider to be one of the best jokes about a non-functioning, non-digital timepiece out there today.

"No, goddammit," he grunted, finally looking up for the first time since I'd been in the place. "I already told you—it's broke."

Since I seemed to have most of his attention at this point, I decided to give my joke another shot, as I was pretty sure he'd get a real kick out of it.

"I know," I said with a wink. "That's why it's only right twice a day!"

I don't think he got it that time, either, even after I giggled at the end to suggest a joke had just been made. And while I'll never understand why, it only seemed to piss him off further, so I decided to ditch the pleasantries and order a Miller High Life, a beer that seemed appropriate, as I've only ever seen it consumed in situations where things weren't really going very well at all.

There was an unattended can of Pabst Blue Ribbon across from me, the owner of which returned from the restroom at about the same time my Miller High Life finally arrived with a damp thud that caused the beer to foam out of the top and across my knuckles as I grabbed it. He was a beefy, bearded fellow in a dirty T-shirt and a leather vest. Gazing into the Budweiser mirror on the wall directly behind him, I could see that there were Hells Angels patches on the back of his vest.

"Things are about to get good," I thought.

I hadn't realized there were any Hells Angels patrolling Cleveland these days, and I was especially surprised to run into one sitting all alone on a Monday night in some lonely bar where Wilson Phillips was blaring, so I figured I should probably take advantage of the situation and try to make friends.

"Does being a biker cause weight gain or is it the other way around?" I wanted to ask him before thinking better of it. Instead I just nodded in that way one does when you're one of three customers sitting all alone in a dive bar in Cleveland on a Monday night. He didn't nod back, but I could tell he saw my nod, which seemed as good an invitation as any to start talking.

"You like Wilson Phillips?" I asked.

"No," he grunted.

"Yeah, me, neither," I said. "Just wanted to make sure."

I was hoping that would be a pretty solid conversation starter, but I quickly realized I should probably try another tack.

"Pretty sweet bike out front," I said. "Yours?"

"Yup," he belched, his lower lip dripping with what I hoped was beer.

"Wouldn't mind getting one like that myself one day," I continued.

"You ride?" he asked, seemingly opening up to me.

"No." I shook my head with a laugh I hoped made me sound both wistful and worldly. "I mean, you know, not so far."

I'd assumed we would have been off to the races at this point, but it quickly became apparent that I was going to have to do a bit more heavy lifting to get this friendship off the ground.

"Couldn't help but notice the vest," I said, as another Wilson Phillips song launched from the jukebox without warning. "You in the Angels?"*

"Yeah," he said, nodding.

"Big fan of their work," I said, nodding back. "Very reputable organization."

---

* I intentionally left off the "Hells" part to sound more familiar and in the know. It seemed like it was worth a shot.

I figured this might be my Hunter S. Thompson moment, when this Hells Angel guy tells me it's totally cool if I roll with him and his friends for a while until they decide to beat the crap out of me one day, thus giving me awesome stuff to talk about at dinner parties and pretty much everywhere else for the rest of my life. But instead he just stared silently at the liquor bottles behind the bar as the Wilson Phillips song came to an end.

"So . . . do you *have* to have a motorcycle to be in the Hells Angels?" I asked him once the next Wilson Phillips song kicked in.

"Yup," he said, now seemingly staring right through the liquor bottles like he was sick of getting asked that question.

"And does it *have* to be a Harley-Davidson?" I continued.

I waited for the answer but it never came. Instead, the lone Angel just grabbed his PBR and walked down to the other end of the bar. I wasn't offended, though. After all, everyone has bad days, even Hells Angels, I bet. And besides, sometimes an outlaw has to go it alone, especially when his one shot at having a decent conversation that might eventually lead to him joining the most infamous biker gang in the world was now across the room trying to make some time with the president of the Cleveland chapter of the Wilson Phillips fan club and it was only a matter of time before his dad realized his car was no longer in the driveway.

Seemingly out of options for human interaction at this point, I decided to take a couple last swigs of my High Life and head back out into the Cleveland night. I tried to kick the door open on my way out of the bar to announce my exit and, by extension, the fact that all three of them in the place had pretty much blown it as far as hanging out with me goes, only to discover that the door opened inward. My toes hurt plenty after that but I was sure to wait until I was at least halfway down the block before letting on even the slightest bit about that.

"'Someday somebody's gonna make you want to turn around and say good-bye,'" I thought, quoting Wilson Phillips lyrics in my head as I searched my jacket for the car keys. "'Until then, baby, are you going to let them hold you down and make you cry?'"

These words had seemed poignant to me before, but never so much as they did right then.

Once back in the Buick, I turned the ignition and pointed the car in the direction of home, figuring that having even half a conversation with a Hells Angel was going to be pretty tough to beat by that point.

I pulled into the driveway back home about twenty-five minutes later, killing the headlights once more before they had a chance to hit the garage door and announce my return in the process. It was creeping up on midnight, so odds were my dad was fast asleep by then anyway. Still, I wasn't taking any chances on rousting him.

After cutting the engine, I stepped out of the car, shut the driver's-side door as quietly as possible, and tiptoed across the pavement toward the side door, only to discover it was locked. I searched the garage for the "secret" house key we usually kept stashed in there, but it was nowhere to be found. I thought to just let myself in the house by tossing a rock through a window or something, but then I realized that that's exactly the sort of thing my dad would pretty much never shut up about, so I gave in to the inevitable and rang the doorbell. It echoed throughout the house, but after thirty seconds or so it became clear that it had failed to produce the desired effect, the one where my dad would get out of bed and let me inside, so I pressed it again. That didn't work, either, so I pressed it again. When that didn't work, I did that thing where you quickly ring the doorbell twenty or thirty times in succession, practically spraining your index finger, until an angry human suddenly appears on the other side of the door, cursing your very existence but, more important, letting you inside anyway so he can go back to sleep. Somehow that failed, too, so I let my desperation get the best of me and pulled my phone out of my pocket with a sigh, to dial the house landline. I heard it ringing inside, and I'm pretty sure the neighbors on either side of the house could hear it, too, but after seven or eight rings, all I got was the machine.

"You've reached the Hill residence," I heard my sister Katy say in a message most likely dating back to the Clinton administration. "Please leave a message."

"Get out of bed and open the damn door, Dad!" I wanted to scream before hanging up instead and calling back nine or ten more times in vain before finally trudging back to the car in defeat.

It occurred to me to just sleep in the car for the rest of the night, but it was pretty cold out, and the thought of having my dad discover my frozen corpse curled up in the backseat at dawn, while admittedly gratifying on some level, ultimately didn't seem worth it. So I fired up the Buick again and begrudgingly drove to the nearby suburb of Beachwood, swearing under my breath the whole way, in search of a hotel for the night. There's a whole strip of them right off the highway there, most of them decent and occupied by families passing through on their way to Chicago, perhaps, or the occasional traveling businessman looking to escape the glitz of downtown Cleveland. But there was also a Super 8 motel in case a drifter or someone on the lam maybe happened to be passing through town at some point and needed a bit of rest just like the next guy. Since it was just me, and my dad would probably be awake and most likely willing to let me back in the house in a few hours anyway, I opted to get a room there. And if I decided to tell my dad about any of this the next day, the idea of me staying at a Super 8 would probably tug at his heartstrings more firmly than if I'd booked myself into the Ramada or one of the other classier establishments on the strip, so it felt like the right move.

I parked out front and walked into the hotel lobby, where I was greeted by a pear-shaped bald man of about sixty wearing thick-framed glasses, a short-sleeve shirt, and a tie that was stained with what appeared to be at least five sauces of unknown origin.

"I'd like a room, please," I told the guy, raising my voice a bit to make sure he heard me through the murky sheet of Plexiglas between us.

"Is it just you?" he asked in a phlegmy baritone that sounded like it hadn't been called to action since the last wrong number at best.

I wanted to tell him it was going to be me and the entire Hawaiian Tropic bikini team, the original lineup of Danzig,* or something else that would really make his ears perk up, but we

---

* I really shouldn't have to explain this, but in case you don't know who Danzig is, they are an excellent heavy metal band whose singer and namesake, Glenn Danzig, just like me, isn't exactly crazy about bullshit. They are the best.

both seemed tired, so I just said yes. Then he rang me up and slipped a key under the Plexiglas like some mechanical fortune-teller at an especially sad amusement park.

"Room 118," he said with a sigh that suggested he'd once had grander plans for himself, and maybe hoped I did, too. "Out the door, to the left, and all the way down 'til you can't go no further."

"You mean until I can't go any farther," I corrected him.

"That's what I just said," he said, staring at me blankly.

As I slowly marched to my room, I thought back to the summer vacations my family used to go on when I was a kid, where all seven of us would sneak into a single room in a motel just like this, everyone but my father ducking down as we drove past the front desk to avoid getting busted by the manager.

"Just pretend you're playing hide-and-seek for a second until I tell you it's okay to stop," my mother would tell us.

I couldn't decide if the fact that it was just me all these years later was progress or not.

Moments later, I pushed open the door to room 118. A heady mixture of stale cigarette smoke, urine, and despair began to fill my nostrils and sting my eyes. I remembered seeing a report on 20/20 or something that said that most hotel rooms were pretty much spackled from floor to ceiling in various bodily fluids. And since I didn't have the energy to do my part in contributing to that statistic, I figured it would probably be best to just tear the covers off the bed and lie down on the sheets fully clothed, shoes and all.

After taking off my jacket to use as a blanket, I curled into the fetal position, plugged my nose, and closed my eyes. As I lay there, I wondered what my mom would have thought of this scene, her own son balled up in the saddest motel room the eastern suburbs of Cleveland had to offer as her husband slept soundly, blissfully unaware that his own son was shivering in the dark in some strange yet reasonably priced bed just a few miles from home. I chose to picture her shaking her head, laughing, as I drifted off to something that resembled sleep. And at some point after that, I had a powerful dream about my mother. I've heard it said by me and at least a few other people that you should never bore someone with stories about your crazy dreams, but, assuming you don't have anywhere to be right now, I'll go ahead anyway:

It was just before dawn and I could hear someone ringing the doorbell to the house.

"Who the hell is ringing the doorbell this early in the morning?" I wondered. It was too early even for some especially determined paperboy to be swinging by or anything.

I walked downstairs to find my mother in her winter coat and hat standing at the side door. And since she was no longer living and all, I was, of course, surprised to see her.

"Sorry it took so long for me to answer the door, Mom," I said. "I was upstairs and didn't hear the doorbell at first."

"It's okay," she said, smiling.

"What are you doing?" I asked her.

"I want to come home," she answered.

"But I thought you were gone," I said.

"I was, but I want to come home now."

Then, for some reason, I decided to walk out into the driveway with my mother rather than head back inside with her. We started walking back toward the garage, where we discovered a fully grown deer lying in the driveway with a broken leg.

"He looks like he's in a lot of pain," my mom said with a grimace.

"Yeah," I agreed.

Then I got down on my knees and began to strangle it in hopes of putting it out of its misery.

"Oh, Davey," my mom said. "Isn't that hard to do?"

"Yeah, but I don't mind doing it if it means you'll stick around."

I guess it was a dream of wishful thinking—both that my mother had returned and that I was sleeping in the house instead of some skanky motel with my shoes still on. And that part about the deer? Yeah, I didn't really get that, either.

Anyway, thank you for indulging me. Now let's get back to room 118.

I woke up a few hours later as the light of dawn began to spill through gravy-colored curtains. I knew my dad was an early riser, so rather than luxuriate any longer at the Super 8, I swung my legs to the side of the bed and stood up slowly like some low-rent Frankenstein before walking out of room 118 and straight to my dad's Buick without even checking to see if a complimentary Continental breakfast was being offered. I probably could have used a cup of coffee for the push home, but instead I just cracked open the car windows and let the crisp, suburban Cleveland air snap me to attention.

I got back to the house a few minutes later to find my dad retrieving the morning paper from the driveway. I had a fleeting impulse to run him over for locking me out of the house the night before, but I realized it was probably just sleep deprivation talking and decided to let the urge pass, as I didn't want to ruin breakfast. Sometimes it's important to keep things in perspective.

"You just getting home from last night?" my dad asked as I stepped out of the car.

"Yeah, I was tired so I ended up crashing at Tim's house," I lied in reference to a friend of mine who had his own house, wife, kid, and other stuff like that. Besides, it occurred to me that it might be better to play the Super 8 card at another time, like if I needed to borrow some cash, for example.

As we stood there, my dad's eyes slowly drifted to the back bumper of his car and his eyes began to narrow.

"Where'd that scratch come from?" he asked, slipping into detective mode.

"What scratch?" I replied.

"That one," he said, pointing his index finger with the same hand he was using to hold the newspaper.

"I think it might have been the Angels," I said, thinking fast.

"What angels?" my dad asked while looking at me like he thought he should probably check me for a fever.

"The Hells Angels," I replied.

"What are you talking about?"

"Well, I wasn't gonna say anything," I began, "but I kind of got into it with a member of the Hells Angels at a bar last night and, while I can't prove anything, that's really the only gang or even individual I can think of that has any sort of beef with me right now, so . . ."

"You got into a fight with a member of the Hells Angels?" he interrupted. I couldn't tell whether he was angry or impressed.

"Sort of," I said. "More of a disagreement, really."

"Where?" he asked.

To be honest, I was curious as to where my story might be headed at this point, too, so I continued.

"Some bar in Ohio City," I told him.

"And this Hells Angel, he scratched my car?"

"I'm not saying that. I'm just saying that if anyone has it out for me right now, it's him."

"Don't you think it maybe could have happened in a parking lot or something?"

"Maybe," I said. "But look at their history—the Hells Angels wouldn't think twice about scratching your car. That sort of thing is business as usual for guys like that. They can be real jerks sometimes. Ask around."

I'm not really sure why I dragged the Hells Angels into things. There was just something nice about feeling wanted or even dangerous for a change, I guess. As for my dad, though, he just seemed confused by this point, so I decided to change the topic entirely before things got worse.

"How'd you sleep last night?" I asked as we both began heading toward the house.

"I was woken up by some nut calling the house over and over again a little after midnight," he answered, "but other than that I slept like a baby."

POWER FOR LIVING

I T WAS THE SUMMER AND I'D DECIDED TO TAKE THE train from New York to Boston to visit my youngest sister, Katy, and her family for the weekend. As I set my bag down in her front hallway, Katy began telling me about how her then-five-year-old son, William, had had a buddy over earlier, and when she told William that I would be arriving later that day, he turned to his friend and said, "You have to meet my uncle David—he's different."

On the face of it, I thought it was a cute enough story, the usual "kids say the darndest things" sort of stuff I usually get a kick out of just as much as the next guy. But deep down inside I found myself thinking, "How in the hell do even small children pick up on this stuff? What am I doing wrong?"

But I guess I should have been used to it by then.

"Your father and I would like to take you to dinner," I remember my mother telling me sometime around my thirtieth birthday, an age by which my siblings all had stuff like jobs and houses and, in some cases, other people had entered into legal agreements to spend the rest of their lives with them, too.

As for me, I was still alternately crashing at my older sister Miriam's place or sleeping in Katy's childhood bedroom, which was right next to my parents' and had remained largely unchanged since her teen years, with the exception of my pants and the occasional empty beer bottle on the floor. It was a pretty solid arrangement as far as I was concerned, but when my mom mentioned the three of us going to dinner, I had a feeling it might have more to do with all the stuff I just mentioned and not because I was the bestest boy in the whole wide world, like I kept trying to tell them.

"We were just wondering if there's anything we can do to help get you further along in your . . . career," my dad explained as we settled into a table in the corner of a restaurant that was way too nice for us to be having dinner at without my also being gently torn a new one.

The fact that even I wasn't sure what "career" he might have been referring to only emphasized this reality. I mean, sure, I'd played in a couple bands that had gotten mentioned in the local papers over the years. And my typing skills had improved dramatically since my sister Miriam started letting me borrow her computer when she wasn't home. But aside from painting a neighbor's bathroom every once in a while or writing the occasional "think piece" to be distributed to friends late at night via e-mail whether they liked it or not, I had spent the past couple years doing what I tend to look back on fondly as "rejecting society" but others tend to look back on not so fondly as "working odd jobs within walking distance of the house while occasionally hitting up family members for cash when at least one of us seemed kind of drunk."

Under the circumstances and also because we had yet to order, it felt like pushing it to answer my dad's question by asking my parents to help me hang flyers for my band's next gig, so when they suggested I might take something called "career testing" at John Carroll University, the local college up the street from our house, I reluctantly agreed. To be honest, part of me was kind of wondering what I was supposed to be doing with my life, too.

The test itself was to be administered by a man named Dr. Nosal, who apparently specialized in helping "free spirits," underachievers, drifters, and other people who tend to live with their parents past the age of thirty get their lives on track or at least get some different roommates. The fact that he was a doctor initially had me worried that electrodes, scanning, and maybe even a bit of probing might be involved with the whole thing, but my dad, noting the look of vulnerability on my face, assured me that most likely wouldn't be the case.

"I doubt you'll even have to take your pants off," he said with a dismissive wave as my double order of crème brûlée arrived. His words gave me comfort.

While I also assumed there would be a whole bunch of us looking to focus on our futures that day, it turned out it would be just me and Dr. Nosal, mano a mano in a room for eight hours straight, not including bathroom or lunch breaks as he administered a variety of tests designed to measure my assorted aptitudes or lack thereof. At the end of it all I would presumably find out exactly why I had been put on this planet, if for some reason it wasn't to melt people's faces, as I'd just assumed up until this point.

As I waited in the lobby of one of the school's many buildings designed for fancy learning, the morning of the test, I was admittedly nervous. It felt like a moment of truth when my actual value as a human being would finally be quantified, written down on a sheet of paper, and, depending on the results, maybe even hung on my parents' refrigerator in between photos of all my nieces and nephews.

"What if it turns out I was meant to be a garbage collector this whole time?" I thought.* "I mean, sure, it would be pretty cool to drive that truck and all but what about those unflattering outfits?"

Before I had a chance to completely freak out, though, a squat man of about seventy, wearing exactly the kind of tweed blazer and knit tie one might expect a guy named Dr. Nosal to wear, slowly poked his head out of a doorway and squinted in my direction.

"David Hill?" he asked. The fact that he used my full name suggested to me that he meant business, that I may very well already be in serious trouble.

---

* I realize some might interpret this sentence as being anti–garbage collector. However, please know that every bit of research I've done into the garbage-collecting industry indicates that if you can get past the smell and avoid being pricked by the odd used syringe, it's actually a pretty sweet gig. In fact, some quick Googling I did between this sentence and the last shows that garbage collectors in New York City make an average of almost $58,000. And that's not including all the cool stuff they must find on their rounds and totally get to keep for free. I bet the sex is pretty good, too.

"Yes," I said, slowly standing up to shake his hand.

I was excited to get the very first question right and figured I was on a roll until we walked into a cramped room with dirty beige walls that felt inconsistent with what I chose to believe would be my bright future, and I realized Dr. Nosal was done with the softballs. There, we both sat down on each side of a long wooden table to let the games begin.

"Let's get down to business," Dr. Nosal said, methodically spreading a few sheets of paper across the table.

It was go time. And while I expected the test would mostly consist of things like his asking me if I liked candy and then putting a check mark next to a box marked "get job at candy factory" if I answered yes (which, for the record, I definitely would have if he'd asked), I couldn't have been more wrong. Instead, Dr. Nosal got things under way with what I'm sure there is a fancier name for—"cognitive" this or that, maybe—but I can only describe as mind games. First, I'd look at a bunch of geometric shapes on a piece of paper and then have to choose which one had actually been a porcupine or some other crazy thing the whole time. Or I'd have to pretend I was the mayor of an imaginary town and decide whether taxpayer money should go toward sexier wheelchair ramps, a statue of the original lineup of Dokken, or maybe a Nazi-themed water park.*

---

* I may not be remembering these questions exactly as they were written, but hopefully you see my point. It was all very confusing. And, for the record, I would never have approved that water park. I do enjoy a good slide, but I am no monster. As for the original lineup of Dokken, I refuse to honor them until they are finally willing to set aside their differences and, in fact, get back to "rockin' like Dokken."

"I see you're ambidextrous," Dr. Nosal noted a few minutes into things as I attempted to solve a puzzle of some sort with my hands.

"I know," I replied, admittedly too embarrassed to explain exactly how.

After what felt like an eternity but turned out to be only a couple of hours, Dr. Nosal announced that he needed to break for lunch. I figured this meant I was slowly wearing him down and he would soon be ready to just give up entirely and walk right out of the building, perhaps never to return, not even to retrieve the fancy plaques suggesting he was qualified to help someone like me in the first place. But when he suggested we go to the Italian place a couple blocks from my house, I realized he was probably just hungry.

"You like pizza?" Dr. Nosal asked, seemingly still in test-giving mode as we slid into a red vinyl booth a few minutes later.

"Yes," I said, convinced that was the right answer. "Spaghetti, too."

I normally love Italian food, but it was hard to enjoy it much this time, as by this point I was convinced that even my pizza-eating methods would be carefully analyzed and later somehow factored into my final test scores. Plus, if any of my friends happened to walk in, how was I going to explain the old dude in the tweed blazer and knit tie sitting across from me?

"You know how I like to hang out in my underwear until around noon and take naps in the middle of the day whenever I feel like it?" I'd say, gesturing to Dr. Nosal. "Well, *this guy* is trying to put a stop to all that."

Like I didn't already have enough problems.

The one bright spot of our lunch break was that Dr. Nosal picked up the tab. I figured he would just tack it onto my final bill, but I never found out for sure because, after a brief powwow, we both agreed my parents should pay for the test since it was their idea in the first place. Also, I think he may have been convinced I was still in high school for some reason and I sure as hell wasn't about to tell him otherwise. Either way, I was really starting to like the guy.

After lunch, we headed back to the college for more rigorous testing that just confused me more than anything else. There were more weird shapes, more tricky questions presupposing I had "values" and then asking me what exactly they might be, and at least a couple more opportunities that I took to mix it up and use my left hand for stuff instead of my right once in a while, something that I'm pretty sure impressed both of us. Occasionally, Dr. Nosal would leave the room, presumably to assess the damage I'd just done on the previous round of questions or perhaps to vent to a colleague in some distant land.

"It's like he was raised by wolves or something," I imagined him sighing into the phone to some other doctor in Switzerland or somewhere equally exotic as he tried to make sense of my handwriting or how I managed to get pizza stains on almost everything even after he insisted I wash my hands before we resumed testing after lunch.

Even so, when Dr. Nosal announced around five p.m. that it was time for us to look at my results, a part of me still hoped he'd discovered I was some sort of mad genius or at the very least entitled to some sort of government assistance. And while neither of those things happened, I assumed this would at least be the part where he wrote down the phone number of some guy who couldn't wait to give me a job in whatever field my test results revealed I was born to dominate. But instead Dr. Nosal just furrowed his brow for a while before telling me that I was best suited to work in "art, music, writing, or entertainment," thus echoing a notion I'd managed to come up with all on my own by the age of seven or so.

"But isn't that why I'm here in the first place?" I asked. "So you can tell what I should do *besides* all that stuff?"

With that, Dr. Nosal furrowed his brow some more and looked down at his papers again.

"Well, you might do okay in the import/export business," he said, which sounded like he was making it up on the spot. "But I'm not really sure about that one."

After a few more parting words, Dr. Nosal shook my hand with a firmness that implied an unspoken "Godspeed!" mixed with a bit of genuine relief that I was finally leaving, and I headed for the door.

On the short walk home, I felt both discouraged and relieved. I was discouraged because I had been convinced that, after a full day of testing, this guy really was going to pretty much tell me where to report for work the next day. But I was also relieved that all those tests had confirmed what I already knew—that I just wasn't cut out for showing up anywhere for work the next day. Unless, of course, there happened to be an import/export operation somewhere in town looking to take a shot on a scrappy young buck like myself. But since he hadn't given me the number for that place, I figured I should probably cross that one off the list.

"How did the testing go?" my dad asked when I walked through the door a few minutes later.

"Yeah, Davey," my mom said. "How did it go?"

Part of me couldn't wait to tell my parents that their plan had backfired and that the test results had only served to confirm their worst fears, that I was completely unemployable, at least in the "real world" they seemed so eager for me to take part in anyway. But instead I just told them what Dr. Nosal told me.

"It turns out I'm best suited for art, music, writing, or entertainment," I said, cringing slightly as I told my parents probably the last thing they wanted to hear.

"But we already knew that," my mom said, careful not to sound too disappointed. "Did he mention anything else you might be good at?"

"The import/export business," I replied.

"Huh?" my mom said.

"Yeah," I said before heading upstairs to my sister's room. "I didn't understand what he meant by that, either."

I supposed I should have been thrilled that even academic testing supported the fact that I wasn't cut out for a "straight job" and that working in a "creative field" was my destiny or, at the very least, the thing I should probably just go ahead and keep whacking at until death comes calling. But when you're pushing thirty and curling up in a twin bed with Holly Hobbie sheets every night in suburban Cleveland, it's hard not to worry at least a little bit. In fact, now that I think about it, that's probably exactly what had my parents so concerned in the first place, too.

As I dozed off to sleep that night, my mind suddenly drifted back to the third grade, when I was somehow convinced I'd one day grow a formidable mustache* and be the boss of a bunch of people in an office somewhere. I even remember drawing a formidable mustache on one of my wallet-sized class photos that year as I imagined grown-up me giving firm yet largely pleasant orders to an assistant I chose to believe was named Donna for reasons that remain a mystery to this day.

"Little Dave Hill really had his shit together," I thought, my feet dangling over the edge of the bed.

For a few days after that, I thought about hopping on the Internet and maybe finding out exactly what the import/export business is, totally getting a job doing that, and—who knows?—maybe even growing a cool mustache, after all. But it didn't take long for me to get back to the original plan of not showing up anywhere for work each morning. After all, an old lack of habits is hard to break. Besides, we only had dial-up Internet back then and it would have taken forever for the pages to load, and I couldn't risk missing my programs while I waited for that to happen.

Despite the occasional flicker of promise in the form of some part-time job or another, not a whole lot changed over the next couple of years until one day I got the wanderlust, went to New York City for the weekend, and ended up staying for good. And as often happens to people not cut out for much of anything else, I got a job writing for a television show and, for a little while anyway, it seemed like I was on my proverbial way. But unfortunately

---

* Please note that while today I write to you as a man fully capable of growing a mustache *and* a beard, I choose to do neither, because, I mean, c'mon—this face!

it didn't take long for the TV show to get canceled and the credit card companies, all of which unfortunately still had me listed as living at my parents' place, to start calling the house again.

"You ever thought about getting a life coach?" my sister Katy called to ask me one day around this time as I sat there wondering whether the beams in my Brooklyn apartment might support a noose.

"A what?" I said.

"A life coach," she replied. "They help you get your life together."

"What are you suggesting?" I asked, trying to muster up the energy to be annoyed.

"Nothing," my sister said innocently. "It just might be helpful to you to talk things through with someone."

"But I already have a therapist."

"A therapist just helps you not be crazy. A life coach helps you get a job and stuff."

A job. There was that word again. Still, as I sat counting the change I'd just found on top of my roommate's dresser, I began to see her point.

As it turned out, Katy's friend had worked with a life coach in Philadelphia who apparently really helped her get her shit together. And when my sister told this story to my mother, presumably without the profanity, she flipped for the idea, so much, in fact, that she even offered to pay the life coach to try to work her magic on me.

"I really don't think it's for me," I told my mom and sister simultaneously on the conference call they had set up to tell me I was about to have a life coach.

"But I'm going to pay for it," my mom said insistently.

"Yeah, and you kind of owe money to everyone in the family, so you can't really say no," Katy added.

All these years later, I still maintain that Katy's logic was flawed, but I guess she wasn't technically wrong, either, so, after whining a bit for dramatic effect, I agreed to more professional guidance.

"After all," I thought, "that Dr. Nosal guy took me for pizza. Maybe this life coach will do fun stuff like that, too!"

The life coach's name was Pam. And since she didn't live in New York City, my coaching would consist of the two of us just talking on the phone for thirty minutes once a week and e-mailing whenever the mood struck. I was pretty excited about this arrangement, as it wouldn't require me to ever leave the house or even get out of bed, really.

"So tell me what you've been up to lately," Pam asked during our first phone session.

I gathered she wasn't asking about my social life, which, for the record, was going great, so instead I told her the part about how I ended up coming to New York for the weekend and never leaving. And then I told her about how I'd gotten a job writing for a TV show that got canceled and also how I was pretty sweet at guitar, and she could ask anyone. By then I'd also begun to try my hand at performing live comedy, so I told her about that, too.

"And what do you do for money?" she asked.

"See, that's where things start to get a little hazy," I said after a long pause.

Don't get me wrong—I was definitely earning *some* money. I'd managed to get some freelance writing gigs here and there. And my cousin Kieran, who managed a bar in Hell's Kitchen, gave me a bartending shift for a few hours each Sunday, a night when business was slow enough to safely put a guy who didn't know how to make a drink that didn't list all the ingredients in the name (e.g., vodka and soda, gin and tonic) in charge of the joint. But things definitely weren't going well enough for, say, a credit card company to let me have one of their fancy cards again or for me to not hide in my bedroom with the lights off whenever my roommate mentioned the rent was due.

As part of getting my life coached, Pam would give me assignments each week, most of which involved my trying to figure out ways to earn money, something I had never been very good at, what with being an "artist" and all. But to her credit, Pam encouraged me to pursue work in entertainment rather than, for example, trying to track down that garbage collector gig I remained conflicted about. She also gave me weekly reading assignments. One book kind of reminded me of *The Secret*, even though I've never actually read that book and ended up mostly freaking me out because it had me convinced I could screw up my future just by thinking about it. The other was by a bearded, New Agey guy who mostly seemed to write about people who walked around wearing sandals and loose-fitting clothing for extended periods, risking dehydration before having epiphanies I could never seem to wrap my head around, for some reason.

A couple weeks into my coaching, my mother asked if she might have a chat with Pam.

"I'm just curious what she does," my mother explained.

"Me, too," I told her before telling her to go ahead and give Pam a jangle.

"I spoke with your mother," Pam told me a few days later during our weekly phone session.

"How did that go?" I asked.

"She's a very nice lady," Pam said in a manner that suggested things didn't go very well at all, something I admittedly got a pretty big kick out of, even though I really liked Pam and was really rooting for her to succeed in getting me to do something with my life.

Shortly after that, Pam happened to be in New York for the day and suggested we meet in person. By this point, she had been coaching my life for a month or two. And while my fortune hadn't changed dramatically, we both at least had a clearer sense of what the hell I did all day, which felt like progress.

I showered and everything in hopes that this was going to be when she'd take me for pizza like Dr. Nosal had, but instead we met in a coffee shop across from Central Park. And as we sat there, I was suddenly struck by the fact that Pam and I were about the same age, something I found at once comforting and horrifying.

"She totally gets me," I thought on the one hand.

"How the hell did I screw up so much that I'm being coached on *life* by someone who hasn't lived any more of it than I have?" I thought on the other.

It kind of messed with my head.

"How's the life coaching going?" my mom asked me shortly after our summit.

"Really well," I said, telling her what I figured she wanted to hear.

"What exactly do you guys talk about?"

"We talk about my goals and how I should think of getting some and maybe even achieve them while I'm at it and, you know, other cool stuff like that, mostly."

"But is she trying to find you a job?" my mom pressed, doing her damnedest to mask any signs of frustration or confusion in her voice.

"It depends what you mean by 'job,' I guess," I said.

I can't remember what my mom said after that but I don't think it was good. I admittedly felt kind of bad about it, too. After all, for what she was paying, she should have at least gotten some pretty cool "before and after" pictures out of the deal, maybe even ones where I'd wind up tucking in my shirt and slicking back my hair and stuff. But it just didn't seem that things were headed that way.

My life got coached for a few weeks more after that. Pam and I would have our regular weekly phone call, which would usually end with some sort of "homework assignment" that involved me having to call someone we agreed could probably buy and sell me ten times over and ask for a job or perhaps just writing up a list of what I perceived to be my "recent accomplishments," or something like that. I was actually starting to enjoy it if for no other reason than for once someone would have to stay on the phone with me for at least a half hour before pulling any of that "Well, I should probably let you go" crap. Sometimes it's just nice to talk, and somehow even more so when it's costing your parents money.

Shortly before our three-month anniversary, my life sensei

told me my mother had asked to talk with her again and she wanted to make sure it was okay.

"Go for it!" I told her.

"It'll be fun for both of them," I thought.

A few days later, I got another call from Pam.

"I have to quit being your life coach," she told me.

"Why?" I asked, assuming I must have really screwed up this time.

"Well, your mother really wants me to talk you into getting a regular nine-to-five job somewhere, but I don't think you should do that," she explained. "And since she's paying me, I can't exactly take her money *and* ignore everything she asks me to do."

"So now what do I do?" I asked, not exactly sure if I had failed or succeeded at having my life coached.

"Just keep doing exactly what you're doing," Pam said. "You're doing fine—you don't need me."

As I sit here in my underwear writing this a decade later, I sure do hope she was right.

And as for my nephew William, I'm pretty sure that little bastard had to put pants on and go to school today. So it looks like I win this round.

THE BACHELOR PAD

I NEVER THOUGHT I'D SEE THE DAY WHEN MY DAD would move into his very own bachelor pad, but then one day it happened—and next thing I know, there I am, totally hanging out with my dad in his bachelor pad, just a couple of dudes in a stalemate over whether to go to Boston Market or not.

"You could get some soup," my dad said, "or a salad or some sweet corn, maybe."

"I could, I guess," I said with a shrug. "I mean, in theory."

"Well, just think about it while I use the restroom real quick," he said.

"Okay," I replied. "See you in an hour."

Anyway, the decision to finally move out of the place my dad had been living in for over forty years came a year or two after my mom died. The family house had suddenly begun to feel too big and quiet, and if somebody ended up leaving the milk out or something, he now had no one to blame but himself. And though his health was still pretty solid for a guy who had been around long enough to remember a world without either television or Velcro, my dad figured it might be good to set up shop someplace new where—in the event that he'd suddenly become trapped under a pile of old newspapers, got lost in the basement, or run out of coffee filters or something—there would always be someone within earshot to hear his screams.

"The only place I'm guaranteed to run into people I know now is at church," he said, "but that's not cutting it anymore."

"Not even with the free donuts?" I asked.

"No, Dave," he said, and sighed, "not even with the free donuts."

It seemed crazy to me, but whatever.

There had been a few discussions about maybe just hiring some sort of part-time nurse to check in on my dad every few days and make sure things were running smoothly within reason, preferably an attractive and fiery young woman from Brazil or somewhere else cool who spoke just enough English to repeatedly ask him when I might be visiting again, but most of those discussions ended with everyone just staring at me for some reason. Eventually my dad began to explore the idea of moving into a retirement community instead, which admittedly made me a bit uncomfortable, as I'd long assumed the phrase "retirement community" was just a euphemism for nursing home, the kind of place you checked into for a few weeks before you were ready to be carted through the back entrance of a funeral home under a bedsheet when no one was looking. After all, here was a man who still drove a car, rode a bicycle, shopped for his own groceries, and was in control of more bodily functions than even I was most days. I was afraid moving into a retirement community might make my dad do what's known in athletic circles as "playing down to the competition" and he'd wind up going downhill much more quickly than if he'd just stayed put in the house.

"Everyone else gets to sit around in diapers all day," he might reason. "Why should I have to be the only one to get up and walk all the way over to the toilet, which—for the record—is in *a whole other room*, every time I need to go?"

"I don't think you need to worry about that," my sister Libby told me.

I decided to anyway, but even so, my dad stayed the course and eventually narrowed his options down to four different retirement communities: one near the family house, one about forty-five minutes away in the town where my sister Libby and her family lived, one run by the Masons, and one that was in some seemingly random town only he seemed to know how to get to with confidence. Personally, I was rooting for the one near the family house because it had a great reputation for around-the-clock care if needed and was also located near a lot of bars I liked, but somehow my dad didn't seem too concerned with either of those things. Libby, of course, was gunning for the one near her house, but—the Waffle House aside—my dad decided there wasn't enough action there for his taste. And while the one run by the Masons sounded promising at first, when my dad and I found out it's actually the Shriners and not the Masons where you get to wear the cool hat and drive around in the tiny car, we crossed them the hell off the list, too. Ultimately my dad opted for the retirement community in the random town.

"It's really great," my dad told me. "They have a restaurant right on the premises and everything."

"You mean a cafeteria?" I asked.

"No, a restaurant," he said.

"You mean anyone can just show up and have dinner there?" I asked.

"No—it's only for residents."

"Sounds like you might still be talking about a cafeteria, then."

"No—it's a restaurant. There are real waitresses and menus, the whole deal. You can even order a martini if you want to."

"I can?" I asked excitedly.

"Not you personally," my dad said, bursting my bubble, "but someone could."

Naturally, I still had a few reservations about the place. And it wasn't just because of that bullshit about the martini, either. But eventually my dad convinced me I had nothing to worry about and that this retirement community wasn't just some place for invalids but was home to all sorts of other people, many of whom had almost no plans of dying anytime soon.

"It really is a neat place," he assured me. "They even have a bunch of activities for the residents here."

"Like what?" I asked.

"Swimming, hiking, horseback riding," my dad said, rattling off a list so long you would have sworn he was reading aloud from a hair-replacement brochure.

"You keep talking like that and I might get a place there myself!" I replied. Then we both laughed because it was so funny.

In the end, my dad got himself a nice one-bedroom apartment

in the retirement community that came with a full kitchen, balcony, and, perhaps best of all, two full bathrooms.

"That way if I'm visiting and we both need to use the bathroom at the same time for any reason whatsoever, everything will be totally fine," I observed. "I can use one bathroom and you can use the other!"

"Yes," he agreed.

We were both super pumped about it.

My dad had been living at his new place a couple months already when I caught a plane back to Cleveland one weekend to pay him a visit. As I pointed my rental car in the direction of his new place, my mind drifted back to old pictures I'd seen of my dad when he was in the Army, years before he'd ever met my mother, when my siblings and I existed merely in the abstract at best and not as the living, breathing beings constantly hitting him up for cash that we'd one day become. There he was, young, slim, and handsome in his enlisted-man uniform, kicking back with a beer in one hand and a cigarette in the other, like his only job during off-hours was to have a good time all the time. I used to giggle at the sight of it, partly because it was hard to believe that my dad had ever been a very young man, but also because I couldn't quite process the idea that he once had a life that had absolutely nothing to do with any of us kids or even our mother, for that matter, that there was a time when he could do whatever the hell he wanted whenever the hell he wanted, and no one could say a damn thing about it. I giggled again as I imagined my dad breaking out the beer and smokes all over again, just picking up all these years later where he had left off, a free man for the first time in almost half a century.

"It's five o'clock somewhere," he'd say, sliding a Pabst Blue Ribbon and a pack of Lucky Strikes across the table at me. "Am I right or am I right?"

It felt strange pulling up to some new address to see my dad after all these years of coming home to University Heights, the town where I grew up. And it felt even stranger to walk into his apartment and see furniture from our family home now arranged in some odd new configuration I feared my mother never would have approved of, complete with what appeared to be at least one or two lawn chairs thrown in for good measure, in a totally new place in some faraway town I'd mostly just heard rumors about while growing up. It was kind of like the final scene in the original *Planet of the Apes* when Charlton Heston is riding a horse on the beach with some smoking hot chick in a tattered loincloth on the back and all of a sudden they happen upon the Statue of Liberty just poking out of the sand—familiar but at the same time all sorts of wrong.

"Ah, damn you! God damn you all to hell!" I thought to say upon discovering he had also dragged a picnic table into the living room. But then I had to admit it did fit in pretty well with the look he seemed to be going for at his new place.

Stranger than any of that stuff, though, was the fact that there was no longer a whole house for my dad and me to hide from each other in. I never realized how much I had taken it for granted. At the old house, I could walk in the side door and set my bag down, and my dad and I could chat for a few minutes in the kitchen before one of us would just wander off midsentence to the basement, a bedroom, or even the attic without explanation before eventually resurfacing to discuss the merits of maybe going to Outback Steakhouse or somewhere else really fun later. Now, aside from excusing ourselves to luxuriate in one of those two bathrooms I was just talking about, there was nowhere for either of us to escape the other should we feel the need. In short, the stakes had been raised.

"So," my dad would say, "your flight was okay?"

"Yeah," I'd answer. "Kind of got screwed on the pretzels, but otherwise fine."

"You're gonna get that every now and again."

"Yeah."

"Uh-huh."

It used to be at this point that I'd run upstairs to stare at my hands or ponder the ceiling in my old bedroom for a while or my dad would mutter something about how he forgot to throw some sheets in the dryer or some other pressing concern, and we could each take off for opposite corners of the house for hours at a time. Now we had to come up with other stuff to say to each other once the conversation about my flight or some other topic of great importance had run its course.

"The balcony is pretty cool," I'd say.

"Yeah," he'd reply.

"Use it much?"

"Sometimes."

"I bet it's pretty fun to stand out there."

"It's not bad."

"Not bad at all, I bet."

"Nope."

"Yup."

It was a lot of work at first. Eventually, though, we got the hang of it, and before long we were chatting back and forth so much you'd have thought we were staging our very own production of *Waiting for Godot*.

But the challenges of my dad's new digs weren't just social. Since he only had one bedroom, that meant one of us would have to sleep in the living room.

"I'll call the front desk and order a cot," my dad said.

"You sure you'll be comfortable on one of those things?" I asked. It was worth a shot.

I probably could have just slept on the couch, but it was the same couch we had in our living room back home while I was growing up and—since we were generally forbidden to even sit on it as kids—I was still pretty sure it would somehow reject my body after all these years and send me catapulting out the window and into the parking lot, where I'd inevitably meet the windshield of any one of the largest four-door luxury sedans I'd ever seen in my whole life. In the end, though, the cot was surprisingly comfortable and I slept pretty well on it. Still, when my dad woke up at his usual five thirty a.m. or so, he decided that even though I was technically sound asleep, since I was in the living room and all, he should probably start talking to me anyway.

"You sleep well?" he asked.

"Until now," I groaned.

"You want some toast?" he asked.

"Maybe later," I said, "like when I'm awake, for example."

I tried to do that thing you're supposed to do with bears where

you close your eyes and lie really still like you're dead and therefore not up for conversation, but it was no use. Eventually I decided to just get up and have some of that toast he wouldn't shut
up about.

"There's coffee, too, if you want some," my dad offered.

"Regular or decaf?" I asked.

"Half-caff," he answered.

"No, thanks. I'll go out for some."

"At this hour?"

In addition to all that, given the tight quarters, it would usually only take a few hours of the two of us hanging out there
together until we were pretty much one raccoon shy of a full-on
Grey Gardens scenario. But like the two Edies, we tried to make
the best of it.

Our quality time together aside, the real perk for my dad in
moving into the retirement community was the opportunity to
interact more regularly with people other than me. To facilitate
mingling, each resident is given a name tag (the one thing I got
right as far as those old Army pictures were concerned, now that
I think about it), which they're encouraged to wear whenever
they decide to wander among the general population.

"Old people aren't always great at remembering names," my
dad explained.

"Can't you just call someone 'dude' or 'man' or 'sugar' or
'toots' or something if you forget a name?" I asked. "That's what
I usually do."

My dad just looked at me after that.

"So are you making friends here?" I said, pressing on.

"Yes," he said. "But it's not easy."

"I imagine a lot of people here are pretty set in their ways and reluctant to meet new people, huh?"

"No. It's just that you meet someone nice here, start to get to know them, and then two weeks later they're dead."

I figured that might be as good a time as any to go for a walk and get a better feel for the place, which, for the record, was crawling with old people. They were literally everywhere. And among the places they liked to frequent most was the flea market on the grounds, where both current and former (i.e., dead) residents can unload whatever items they no longer have use for. It's mostly the kind of stuff you might expect—used oven mitts, coffee mugs, and shellacked wooden plaques with whimsical sayings either carved or painted onto them in equally whimsical fonts, but there's also a section for the more tech-savvy consumer where just about any gadget that was state-of-the-art in 1985 or before is available at a price so low it seems like a trap.

"Pretty cool answering machine," I said to the lady sitting behind a tablecloth-covered card table at the entrance.

"If you like it, I can throw in the original minicassettes for free," she said, sweetening the pot.

"Put that down," my dad said, noting the glimmer of excitement in my eye.

"What if someone calls?" I asked as he began moving toward the exit.

I momentarily had my eye on a pillow with a hunting scene that harked back to a simpler time crocheted into it, but in the end I decided to pull the trigger on a floppy disk priced to move at twenty-five cents. My dad ended up not buying anything at all.

But I guess when you have daily access to a treasure trove like this, you can afford to play it cool.

"What are you gonna do with that floppy disk?" my dad asked me as we headed back to his apartment.

"'What *aren't* I going to do with this floppy disk?' is the question you should be asking," I told him. "Then it would take me less time to answer."

He just looked at me after that, too.

Meanwhile, back at the apartment, my dad and I began our usual debate over what to do about dinner.

"We could go to the restaurant they have here," he offered.

Again with the damn restaurant. I still didn't feel quite ready to take the plunge. Given the clientele, I assumed the food would probably be pretty bland and maybe even sent spinning through a blender a couple times to eliminate the need for chewing at any point. And I could already hear all the questions people my dad's age tend to ask me, like whether or not I "have a job" and what I "do for a living." I thought to suggest we swing by the Mexican restaurant in town instead, where I knew I probably wouldn't get hassled, but as best I could tell my dad had already grown pretty attached to that name tag of his. With all the changes that had been going on, the last thing I needed was for some stranger to just walk up and address him by his full name when we were just a couple of guys looking to eat some goddamn quesadillas without incident.

"Fine," I said. "Let's go to the restaurant."

My dad grabbed his cane, which I tended to think was more of an affectation than something he actually needed to get around, and we headed for the skyway down the hall from his apartment.

"These things are wonderful," he said, waving his arms around like Willy Wonka giving a tour of his chocolate factory. "I can go all the way from my apartment to the restaurant without ever having to go outside."

"The future is now," I said with as much enthusiasm as I could muster.

As we entered the main building with the restaurant, my dad ran into various residents he'd become acquainted with since moving in.

"Hi, Carl," my dad said to some guy in a maroon sweater who was apparently named Carl.

"Hi, Bob," Carl replied without even looking at my dad's name tag. It was impressive.

"That guy's wife had some sort of illness and now she can't speak," my dad told me once Carl was out of earshot.

"Does that make it hard for them?" I asked.

"No," he said. "They get along great."

A few steps later, we ran into a gray-haired woman named Joan.

"Hi, Bob," Joan said. "Who's this?"

"This is my son David," my dad told her.

"He looks like you," Joan said, somehow looking directly at my face without looking me in the eye, "except fatter."

"She seems nice," I said to my dad as we continued on our way.

"You can't listen to what some of the people here say sometimes," my dad said, trying and failing to make me feel better.

We managed to make it just a few more feet before another woman, who looked to be about eighty, told me she had the same nautical-themed sweater I happened to be wearing at the time.

I resented the implication that I was dressed like an old lady, but as I looked down at my stretch-fabric navy slacks and spotless white canvas sneakers, I realized she kind of had my number.

"My daughter knitted my sweater for me," the lady explained, "so they're not *exactly* the same."

Now she was just being a jerk. It was at this point I decided to start taking my dad's advice about not listening to people here.

Meanwhile, at the restaurant entrance, my dad ran into another guy he knew who was wearing a full tuxedo.

"Hi, Bob," the guy in the tux said.

"Hi, Ron," my dad replied. "This is my son David."

"Nice to meet you, David," he said, shaking my hand like he was running for office.

"Nice to meet you, too, sir," I replied, smiling at him with my big fat face.

Presumably in the interests of forced socialization and not making the waiters have to run around as much, the staff at the restaurant seats people together at tables whether they really know each other or not, so when my dad asked for a table for two, we were led to a table shared with a couple with whom my dad seemed at least vaguely familiar.

"This is my son David," my dad said as we pulled our chairs in.

"I'm Janice," the woman said, half smiling and squinting through her bifocals, "and this is my husband, Gary."

Gary nodded slightly but seemed to be focused mostly on his corn.

A couple minutes later, our waitress came by with some menus. My dad and I took a quick glance and we both decided to order some kind of meat with some kind of gravy.

"Do you have children?" my dad asked the couple.

"We have a son and a daughter in Michigan," Janice answered.

"I like Michigan," I chimed in, just trying to heat things up. "Ann Arbor, Detroit, some of the other places . . ."

"David lives in New York," my dad said, nodding in my direction.

"Oh," Janice replied before momentarily turning her attention back to Gary and his corn, which—as long as we're on the topic—he was having a really tough time with. "And do you have any children?"

"No," I said. "I mean, not that I know of."

I waited for the big laugh that usually follows a really great joke like this, but it never came, not even from my dad, who I was pretty sure had really seemed to enjoy it in the past.

It was at this point that I thought to try and order one of those martinis I'd heard about when my dad wasn't looking, but instead we just finished our dinner without incident and began the short trek back to his apartment. On our way out of the restaurant, I noticed Ron, the guy in the tuxedo from before, seated at a table with a couple of other old people, both of whom appeared to be wearing what some cultures might refer to as pajamas. I had assumed earlier that Ron must be on his way to some sort of gala or another, but now realized he probably just had an "anything goes" approach to life, the kind whereby if you feel like putting on a tuxedo for dinner at your retirement community even though no one else is wearing a tuxedo, you go ahead and do it and don't give a crap what anybody else thinks. The more I thought about it, the more I liked the cut of his jib.

"Do you ever wear a tuxedo to dinner?" I asked my dad as we continued walking.

"No," he said. "No, I don't."

Even now I'm not entirely sure whether I was disappointed or relieved by that answer.

When we got back to my dad's apartment a few minutes later, we ran into a white-haired woman, wearing a tracksuit and pearls, in the hallway. My dad introduced us and I did the usual simultaneous nodding and smiling politely maneuver I'd mastered for such occasions. And as I did so, all of sudden I found myself having flashbacks of visiting my grandparents at their apartment building back when I was a kid. Normally this would have been the point when I might be offered some candy or cookies or even told how she has a grandson just about my age. But then I remembered this woman probably just saw me as some random grown man hanging out with his dad, and not as the most adorable boy in the whole wide world or anything. And suddenly it occurred to me that maybe the real reason I had such hang-ups about my dad moving into this place wasn't because I was worried it might hasten his own aging process, but because it reminded me way too much of the fact that someday I, too, would be in the winter of life, a hunched-over old man, no doubt scrambling frantically to find out if those Shriners had opened up a retirement community of their own yet.

When I got back to my apartment in New York the next night, I fixed myself a martini in the biggest glass I could find. I don't care for them much, but I finished it anyway. And that floppy disk made one hell of a coaster.

MEXCELLENT

LIFE CAN BE PRETTY CRAZY SOMETIMES. ONE MINUTE you're lying around in your underwear in your apartment in New York City while getting verbally smacked around by that Suze Orman, the next you're deep inside the bowels of a Mexican prison, drenched in sweat and surrounded by inmates as you pluck away on a beat-up old guitar as fast as your fingers will carry you. At least that's what happened with me anyway.

Here's how it all went down.

I was flipping through the *New York Times* one Sunday when I stumbled across an article about my old friend Bob. Back when I was a pretty young thing attending Fordham University in the Bronx, Bob was on the faculty as part of the school's campus ministry department. Ostensibly his job was to help get students pumped about the idea of showing up for Mass on Sundays and, who knows, maybe even cracking open a Bible every once in a while, too, but he also went out of his way to do things like make sure guys like me, who were perhaps more interested in rocking out wherever and whenever possible, had somewhere to hold band practice each week and even a place to play shows whenever we felt the need to melt faces in a public forum, whether that was a good idea or not. In short, he was a pretty cool dude.

I'd lost track of Bob after graduation, and it turned out that since I'd last seen him he'd packed his bags for Mexico and become a Roman Catholic priest in Saltillo, a town in the northeastern state of Coahuila that rarely factors into the travel plans of Americans on account of all the murdering, kidnapping, carjacking, and other surefire vacation ruiners that tend to be business as usual in those parts. Bob's main gig down there was as a chaplain in the local prison, a job that had become even less fun than it sounds after cartel members inside the prison went and killed the warden one day. It was a dick move by all accounts, but apparently the Mexican government was still impressed enough with the job that from that day forward they pretty much let the cartel run things inside the prison, while keeping their own "official guards" on the outside in case anything really insane happened. The place had essentially become a Mexican Thunderdome, but Bob kept showing up for work every day anyway. Like I said, a pretty cool dude.

I decided to drop Bob a line on Facebook,* we got to chatting, and I eventually asked him if I might pop down Saltillo way for a visit. I've always had a thing for prisons and I love Mexican food, so when Bob hinted that the trip would be all-inclusive, it seemed crazy not to go.

"I can't promise you nothing will happen," he warned me.

---

* Yes—even Catholic priests in Mexican prisons are on Facebook. Happy now, Zuckerberg?

"But things have been a bit calmer down here lately, so you'll probably be fine."

Despite Bob's ringing endorsement, when I told friends of my vacation plans, they tried to talk me out of it altogether.

"You'll be beheaded," they suggested in addition to some other, more negative stuff.

The U.S. State Department website wasn't very encouraging, either, going on about "deferring all non-essential travel," presumably even if you haven't seen your friend Bob in a seriously long time. But when I mentioned the trip to my brother,* he couldn't have been more supportive.

"You'll have the time of your life," he assured me, "and if anything happens, you won't care because you'll be dead."

It was all I needed to hear, and with that I hopped the next plane. I couldn't wait to get down there and start soaking up the fun. During a layover at the Houston airport, I decided to give Bob a ring to let him know I was on my way.

"Great," Bob said. "It'll be you, me, and a recently released inmate staying at my place—he's a murderer-rapist."

For a second, I wondered how a murderer-rapist winds up getting out of prison and crashing at Bob's place like that, but then figured that any murderer-rapist good enough for Bob was good enough for me, and I shouldn't let myself get too bent out of shape about it. Besides, Bob hung up before I had a chance to ask any follow-up questions. Sometimes you just gotta keep moving.

A couple hours later, my plane touched down in Saltillo. The

---

* Also named Bob.

airport there was tiny, looking more like a bus station, really, except for all the planes outside.

I made my way across the tarmac and inside to customs, where, as the only gringo, I'm guessing I stuck out. The customs officials apparently agreed and pulled me aside for additional screening/groping, probably because of my rock look but possibly just to break the day up a bit, too.

Once the customs guys finished having their way with me, I spotted Bob waiting for me at the entrance. Aside from some gray in his beard and the cane at his side, he looked exactly as I'd remembered.

"*Hola,*" he said, offering his hand.

"Hey, Bob," I said, offering mine.

"This is Manuel," Bob continued, gesturing to the mustachioed twentysomething standing next to him. "He's staying with me at the house right now."

"Ah . . . the murderer-rapist," I thought to reply. But I didn't want to get off on the wrong foot or seem like I had hang-ups about that sort of thing, so instead I offered my hand and said, "*¡Hola!*"

As is often the case when you say hello in Spanish to a Spanish-speaking person in a Spanish-speaking country, Manuel immediately started talking to me in Spanish. But after I explained to Bob that "*¡Hola!*" was about as good as it got as far as my Spanish went, Bob mumbled something in Spanish to Manuel, and from then on Manuel mostly just smiled and nodded at me, as it turned out his English was about as good as my Spanish. I tried to remind myself that 90 percent of all communication is nonverbal, but it was honestly hard to tell what either of us was really thinking at that point.

As we rolled toward town in Bob's beat-up hatchback, I was surprised to find that the outskirts of Saltillo didn't look that much different from, say, the outskirts of Akron, Ohio, on an especially balmy day.

"People think it's going to be all sombreros and strolling mariachi bands as far as the eye can see down here," Bob explained as we drove by fairly standard-looking strip malls, gas stations, and the like, "but it's not really like that."

"Bummer," I thought, nodding like I was okay with all of that.

A few minutes later, Bob, Manuel, and I found ourselves on the streets of downtown Saltillo, and after a quick lap around the town square, where teenagers flirted around a boombox blaring what sounded like the Mexican equivalent of Rihanna, we made our way to a Mexican restaurant that Bob suggested was pretty Mexcellent without actually using that word.

"*¡Cerveza!*" I yelled at our waiter as soon as we were seated.

Bob and Manuel seemed pretty impressed that I'd managed to break out a second Spanish word from out of nowhere like that. So when our beers arrived a couple minutes later, I raised mine in a toast and yelled "*¡Cerveza!*" a couple more times while I was at it. Bob and Manuel smiled and clinked their beers with mine, but as I quickly learned, you can only yell "Beer!" in Spanish so many times before people start to think you have a problem.

A few minutes later, a massive platter of fajitas arrived at our table. As I began stuffing my face with abandon, I imagine Bob and Manuel were kind of relieved I was unable to speak, at least for a little while anyway. But when Manuel excused himself to go to the bathroom, I took a break from my gluttony to address a mild concern.

"So, Bob," I said as nonjudgmentally as possible, "how does a murderer-rapist end up just getting out of prison and joining us for fajitas like this?"

What with Manuel's lack of English skills and all, I'm not sure why I waited for him to leave to inquire about his criminal status, but in the event that he actually was a murderer-rapist, I figured I probably shouldn't take any chances.

"I was kidding—he's just a thief," Bob said, smiling. "But definitely let me know if any of your stuff goes missing while you're here."

The next morning, after hiding all of my stuff in various cracks and crevices around the room Bob had given me to stay in, I joined him in running a few errands around town, the first of which involved dropping off a couple of pizzas at the prison for an inmate who was celebrating a birthday that day with a pizza party. It's not often enough that you hear the words *pizza*, *prison*, and *party* all in the same sentence like that, so I was understandably excited as it sounded like a recipe for instant good times as far as I was concerned. But when we got to the prison, I was in for a bit of a letdown.

"You only have permission to come inside the prison tomorrow," Bob told me outside the main entrance. "You're gonna have to wait here until I get back."

"Oh . . . sure . . . yeah . . . that's totally fine," I lied to Bob. "You go have fun and I'll just be right here sitting all alone outside of a Mexican prison. As one does."

As Bob headed inside with the pizzas, I took a seat and sulked quietly on a bench out front. There, as prison guards clad in bulletproof vests casually strolled past on their rounds, I watched cars (and the occasional black pickup truck with gun-toting Federales perched in the back) whiz by in the hot sun along a stretch of elevated highway about thirty yards in front of the prison. I was starting to doze off when Bob appeared outside the gate once more.

"Let's go," he said.

"How was the pizza party?" I asked, shaking off the tired.

"Really good."

"I'll bet."

As Bob and I headed back to his car, I became curious about the guards I'd seen out front.

"Hey, Bob," I asked, "why do the guards wear bulletproof vests when they're *outside* the prison?"

"Oh, *that*," Bob said as if I had been inquiring about a wacky refrigerator magnet or something. "People drive along that highway over there and shoot people in front of the prison sometimes."

"But, Bob," I said, "*I* was just sitting in front of the prison for twenty minutes."

"It's Saturday," Bob said with a shrug. "It's not really a big day for that."

I didn't find his answer all that satisfying. But, not wanting to seem difficult, I decided to just roll with it and climbed back into the passenger seat of his Chevy, like the odds of me getting randomly shot in front of a Mexican prison weren't very good at all. I didn't want Bob to think he'd wound up in one of those scenarios where you haven't seen a friend in a long time and when you finally reconnect, you learn he's turned into a real complainer and isn't nearly as fun as you remembered.

Part of Bob's job is to check in on guys who have been recently released from the prison. So, from the prison pizza party, Bob and I went to visit Geronimo, another former inmate who lived downtown in an apartment owned by his mother. Geronimo is at least six and a half feet tall, which is pretty big for a Mexican guy—or really anyone, the more I think about it. But perhaps more striking than his height was the fact that Geronimo's face was crudely tattooed with images of Bugs Bunny and Speedy Gonzales on each cheek.

"Why does Geronimo have tattoos of Bugs Bunny and Speedy Gonzales on his face?" I asked Bob once I was pretty sure Geronimo didn't speak English, either.

"He really likes Bugs Bunny and Speedy Gonzales," Bob answered.

Again, it didn't quite seem like a good enough explanation to me, but after that thing about people driving along the highway to shoot people in front of the prison, I was ready to let pretty much anything slide. Besides, those face tattoos were the least of Geronimo's problems.

Apparently, another former inmate named Chilango had been crashing at his place the past few days and, just the night before, went and had sex with a prostitute right in Geronimo's bed.

"That's just rude," I told Bob when I heard the news.

Bob translated what I said to Geronimo and Geronimo smiled at me with a look that seemed to say, "I know, right?!" It was nice to connect with him like that.

"You get yourself a prostitute, you have sex with her in your own bed—that's just manners," I wanted to tell him before thinking a priest probably shouldn't have to translate sentences like that.

As it turned out, Geronimo wasn't the only one who had been burned by Chilango. Apparently Chilango had been staying with Bob until just a few days prior. Like Manuel, Chilango had moved in with Bob after getting an early release from the hoosegow, and during that time threw several parties at Bob's place, had prostitutes over on more than one occasion (a "thing" with him, I guess), and even brought home a puppy one day, despite the fact that Bob already had a dog. Part of me couldn't help but admire Chilango's joie de vivre, but when Bob told me Chilango had also stolen the equivalent of four hundred dollars from him while he was at it, I supported Bob's decision to tell Chilango to hit the bricks. The other stuff—sure, I could see it. After all, a guy's gotta live his life. But stealing that kind of cash from your roommate? That's crossing a line.

Despite the relatively unorthodox circumstances of my trip, I was having a good time and, in fact, was really starting to enjoy what turned out to be a much-needed vacation.

That night back at the house, Bob, Manuel, and I relaxed over a few beers. And even though I couldn't help but use it as another opportunity to practice saying *hola* and *cerveza* perhaps a few too many times, they both seemed slightly less annoyed, as at least they had the option of going into their bedrooms and shutting the door behind them if it got to be too much. Still, when I told Manuel I had met Geronimo, making a gesture to suggest I found him unusually tall, his smile of recognition felt like progress.

. . .

I could barely sleep that night in anticipation of my trip to prison the next day. But that didn't matter much because, as I found out the hard way the night before, pretty much everyone in Mexico has a couple of roosters in their yard, so sleeping in past five a.m. or so is next to impossible anyway. I tried to lull myself back to sleep by fantasizing about slowly strangling every rooster in the neighborhood one by one, the life slowly draining from their soft, feathery bodies, but it was no use, so I eventually dragged myself out of bed and joined Bob in the kitchen for a cup of coffee as we geared up to go to prison.

"Since you can't speak Spanish, you should probably play guitar whenever possible once we get inside," Bob told me on the short drive over. "You *really* want the inmates to like you."

"Duh," I thought before imagining what might happen if the inmates didn't like me and scouring my pockets for a spare guitar pick. I also wondered what Bob, who wore black jeans and a gray golf shirt instead of traditional priestly attire, might use for backup should he ever need it.

"Wouldn't you be a little safer around here if you dressed like a priest?" I asked him.

"If I have to dress like a priest for people to know I'm a priest, then I'm not doing my job," Bob replied, staring at the road ahead.

It was at this point that I thought about telling Bob how he sounded like a badass. And that I felt like kind of a wuss by comparison. But I figured he already knew both of those things.

The men's prison in Saltillo is hard to miss—it's a large and weirdly pink building with the word CERESO, Spanish for "prison," painted in giant black letters on one wall. As it came into view from a couple blocks away, I couldn't help but feel a little scared. This was the day I'd be going inside.

"The climate here has been a bit more peaceful lately," Bob told me.

I figured "peaceful" was a fairly relative term when it came to prison, so when Bob had stopped the day before at a religious-supply store to pick up some hosts, the small breadlike wafers used in Catholic communion, I bought an inexpensive crucifix to wear around my neck for a little added protection. As Bob pulled into the prison parking lot, I made sure the crucifix was hanging outside my collar in hopes that it might underscore the "I'm with Bob" vibe I felt might be good to put out there once we got inside.

After parking the car, Bob and I made our way past the fence that surrounds the prison, where we were greeted by a guard wielding an automatic rifle and wearing Lynyrd Skynyrd arm-bands emblazoned with the Confederate flag.

"Skynyrd," I said, nodding in approval. "Cool."

"Are you a redneck?" he asked me in perfect English.

I was taken aback by his question and thought to explain to him that Lynyrd Skynyrd is a very popular southern rock band whose music—especially their pre–plane crash output—is enjoyed by all sorts of people in America, but instead I told him that, yes, I was, in fact, a redneck who followed the band closely to this day and tried to stay as close to Bob's side as possible as we continued toward the prison. I also thought about how the guys in Lynyrd Skynyrd would probably be happy to know they have fans pretty much everywhere.

Once we got to the main gate, Bob presented another guard with a letter granting me permission to go inside. The guard quickly scanned the letter before glancing in my direction and casually waving us inside as if today were the annual "Take Your Friend Whom You Haven't Seen in a Seriously Long Time to Work at a Mexican Prison Day" and he was totally used to this sort of thing.

Inside, Bob was immediately greeted by just about everyone in sight, like he was Norm walking into Cheers at happy hour. I tried saying *"¡Hola!"* followed by a nod in Bob's direction as if to say, "Don't hassle me—I'm with him," but I don't think anyone even noticed me as Bob was clearly a star in these parts. I wasn't surprised—not only is Bob a great guy, but as far as places where people are looking to get in touch with a higher power go, prison tends to be pretty high on that list, so I imagine a guy like Bob can't stop by often enough.

After passing through another series of steel gates, Bob and I entered the prison courtyard, a dirt field where the prison's general population mingled with visiting family members. Despite the largely negative advance press I'd read about the place, it didn't look that bad at first, almost resembling a town square in some small, out-of-the-way village. But as my eyes scanned farther, the barbed-wire fences, watchtowers, and other stock prison trappings came into view and I was quickly reminded exactly where I was.

"¡Pesos! ¡Pesos!" almost every inmate I made eye contact with whispered to me as I passed in hopes that I might hand over whatever spare cash I had on me. Since I'd left my wallet in Bob's car, I just shrugged and held my empty palms up at my side, the

international symbol for "Sorry, dude—I got nothing," and kept walking.

The prison chapel was located just off the courtyard and inmates had already begun filing in for Sunday Mass. Their punctuality was noteworthy to me as, in my experience, people tend to roll into church for Mass at the last possible moment if they show up at all, presumably so they can keep the time spent from the rest of their lives as brief as possible. But I guess when the rest of your life is prison, that sort of thinking is easily reversed.

The walls inside the chapel were a light peach color, having recently been painted by resident cartel members after they'd gotten word that a rival cartel had built an entire church for another priest a few towns over. It was a "keeping up with the Joneses" sort of move that Bob had no choice but to go along with.

"You can't really say no to the cartel guys when they offer to do something," Bob explained somewhat ominously, "so I just had them paint it the same color it was before."

To be fair, I wasn't looking for any trouble either, so after Bob disappeared into the church sacristy to put on his vestments, I grabbed a beat-up nylon-stringed guitar that had been sitting unattended on the floor next to the altar. There were a handful of inmates with guitars gathered to serve as the choir during Mass, so I held the guitar up in their direction as if to ask "Is it cool if I sit in with you guys?" They didn't react one way or another, so I took that as a yes and pulled up a chair next to them. And as I sat there with the guitar, I felt the unmistakable comfort that holding a guitar has always given me.

"Who cares if I'm in a Mexican prison?" I thought. "If anyone hassles me, I'll just play something off *Double Live Gonzo!*, and

I'm sure everything will be fine." That had always worked for me in the past. Why should today be any different?

A couple minutes later, Bob appeared on the altar in a bright green robe. On the chest was sewn a large silver cross, the bottom of which was made to look like the business end of a key. Bob once worked as a graphic artist in New York City, and had come up with the design himself. The message was something along the lines of "the Lord shall set you free from these prison walls." I sure hoped he was right. Either way, it looked pretty cool.

A few moments later, Bob began the Mass. The choir kicked in on cue, but since I didn't know any of their repertoire, I just took a guess at the key they were playing in and chimed in with some occasional guitar noodling* on top of their chord progressions whenever I felt like we needed to take things to the next level in the name of a power greater than all of us put together.

I've attended literally thousands of Catholic Masses over the years, so even though this one was in Spanish, it was easy for me to follow along and fall into the usual pattern of sitting, standing, kneeling, and making the occasional sign of the cross as if on divine autopilot. When I was a kid, my family would go on vacations together and stop in for Mass at a Catholic church in town wherever we happened to be on that given Sunday. This didn't feel all that different except for the fact that my sisters weren't here trying to make me giggle and I was worried some of these dudes maybe wanted to kill me.

Shortly after communion, Bob gestured toward me while say-

---

* Also known as "heat" or "sauce," if you hang out with me anyway.

ing something in Spanish that ended with my name, which I took to be my cue to start melting faces. Since we were in church, though, I tried to keep things under control, maybe even a little Christlike, and instead just improvised a short instrumental piece that I'd like to think went over pretty well, since no one shanked me or did anything else that might be interpreted as negative at any point during the performance.

Once Mass was finished, Bob headed back to the sacristy to hear confession, and I remained in the chapel with a handful of inmates, smiling dumbly, not entirely sure what to do next. Fortunately, one of my fellow choirmates broke the awkward silence by strumming a few chords, over which I began to solo along with him at a fairly blistering speed, partly because I can and partly because I was still kind of scared.* And since Mass was over, I figured there was no reason to hold back anymore. To do so would be what's known in biblical circles† as "hiding your light under a bushel." And as best I could tell, prison just didn't seem like the kind of place to go pulling that kind of crap.

Before long, inmates began to wander in from the courtyard to

---

* Sometimes playing really fast, or "shredding," as it is also known, is frowned upon by music fans, as they consider it to be in bad taste. But the important thing to realize is that when guitarists play really fast, they aren't showing off—they're just kind of scared. Yngwie J. Malmsteen, Joe Satriani, even Eddie Van Halen—they're all just kind of scared. Go easy on them, okay? Life is short—we gotta take care of each other.

† Specifically the Gospels of Matthew, Luke, and John. I got curious and looked it up. Don't worry, though—I did not pick up an actual Bible. I just looked it up on Wikipedia to ensure this book would remain a secular text for all to enjoy. Everything is going to be fine.

hear the strange gringo from Cleveland practically set everyone's hair on fire with his scorching hot licks that, had I not already been playing them behind bars, probably would have landed me in jail. And while none of the inmates seemed to speak much English, one of them knew enough to look me dead in the eye and utter those two words I long to hear whenever a guitar is near: "Hotel California." Naturally, I didn't miss a beat and the version I played that day would have given Glenn Frey and Don Henley a run for their money in even their most drug-addled years.

I have no idea what the inmates said to me when I finished, but it seemed positive. And when Bob walked out of the sacristy about forty-five minutes later, I was in no hurry to leave, as by this point I was pretty sure it was good times all the time when you're jamming on Eagles tunes in a Mexican prison. I had at least five more of their biggest hits locked and loaded, too. Still, Bob was my ride home, so when he said it was time to go, I reluctantly set down the guitar, backed away from it like it was in flames, and followed him out of the chapel.

As we walked toward the exit, I asked where the cartel members I'd heard so much about were hanging out that day.

"They're over there," he said, gesturing toward a small cinder block building in the middle of the courtyard that housed the prison taco stand.* I noticed a web address had been prominently painted on the wall outside along with Twitter and Facebook handles.

---

* I know—I couldn't believe they had one of those in prison, either. And for the record, not that anyone's keeping score, but "prison taco stand" is right up there with "prison pizza party," as far as I'm concerned.

"Does the prison taco stand really have an Internet presence?" I asked.

"No," Bob answered. "The cartel guys just think that's funny. They painted the outside of the prison store to look like an Oxxo, the Mexican equivalent of 7-Eleven, too."

"That's pretty good," I said, laughing.

"Yeah," Bob replied. "The cartel guys can be pretty horrible, murderous people at times, but I have to admit they have a really good sense of humor."

It's always strange to hear about the lighter side of otherwise evil men. You'd think it would just be killing and maiming all the time with guys like that, but everyone requires a bit of balance in life, I guess. For example, did you know Hitler had a pet dog named Blondi that he was apparently crazy about? He ended up feeding the poor dog cyanide one day, but up until that point it's my understanding that they had nothing but fun together.

When Bob and I got back to the house that evening, Manuel and Bob's friend Jorge, who was visiting from Monterrey, stood waiting in the driveway. I'm guessing it might have had something to do with that thing about Manuel being a thief, but for whatever reason he didn't have his own set of keys to the place, so Bob had to let him back in each night.

Once we got inside, we all sat down in the living room to chat over beers. Fortunately for me, Jorge was fluent in English, so I was able to dispense with my usual smiling and nodding and engage in some actual conversation.

It was past sunset, but it was still hot as hell outside, so Manuel took off his shirt, revealing a series of crude tattoos on his arms and shoulders. There was one of the grim reaper and then a couple that weren't quite so grim. But none of them were as whimsical as the ones Geronimo had on his cheeks. I still can't decide whose I liked better.

After a few minutes, Manuel's cell phone rang and he got up to take the call outside as Bob, Jorge, and I continued to chat and drink beer. A short while later, he reappeared in the living room, clearly freaking out about something or other, not that I understood a word of it.

"What's up with him?" I asked Bob and Jorge.

"Chilango called and said Manuel owes him three hundred pesos, the equivalent of about twenty-five dollars," Bob explained. "And if he doesn't pay him back he's going to come to the house, kill me and Jorge, trash the house, and steal my car."

It sounded like none of my business, but I couldn't help but inquire further. As the story goes, Chilango had bought beer for Manuel and himself with the money he'd stolen from Bob and was now insisting that Manuel pay him back for his share of the beer. He was apparently being a real dick about it, too. A reasonable person would stop at the murdering, I thought. But no—Chilango has to go and make a mess of the place and steal Bob's car while he's at it. It was all a bit much, if you ask me.

"So, uh, Manuel's gonna give him the money, right?" I asked.

"No," Bob said, shaking his head between sips of beer. "If Manuel pays him, it's just going to show Chilango that this tactic is effective."

"It sounds pretty effective to me," I said, my voice cracking a bit, "especially the part about how he's going to kill you guys—I don't know about you but that part really made my ears perk up."

"I'm not afraid of Chilango," Jorge told me. "You wanna know why?"

"Definitely," I answered.

"Because I'm not afraid to die," Jorge said, leaning toward me for emphasis like they do in those movies where the guy who says stuff like that ends up getting killed at some point later in the movie.

"You know what? Why don't you guys let me get this one?" I offered. "It's the least I could do."

"No one's going to pay Chilango anything," Bob said, laying down the law in his usual soft-spoken yet entirely effective way.

"Yeah, that makes sense," I said, trying to go along with the plan, or lack thereof, and just get back to enjoying everyone's company during the time we had left together. "After all, if the guy doesn't even have a spare twenty-five bucks, I'm sure he can't afford a gun to come over here and kill you guys with anyway."

"This is Mexico," Bob reminded me. "People use machetes down here—it's more dramatic."

Suddenly my mind drifted to the telenovelas I had seen on Spanish television and how everyone seemed to be screaming way more than on just about every other channel that came with my cable package. Maybe this would be kind of like that, only instead of some busty beauty getting angry with everyone and storming out of the room, it would just be this Chilango guy showing up at the house with a machete and looking really miffed.

"Are you sure I can't just pay Chilango the money?" I asked again in an attempt to refocus things. "I'd really love to, the more I think about it. Think of it as a mitzvah!"

"That's okay," Bob said.

"Do you think it's just an idle threat?" I pressed.

"Yeah," Bob replied as he stood up and headed for bed. "Then again, you only get one chance to be wrong about that sort of thing."

For his part, Manuel just sat there, still shirtless and sweating profusely as he sipped his beer and stared intently at what I could only assume was a gory vision of the increasingly near future. I began to do a bit of thinking myself, and it occurred to me that if and when Chilango was to swing by with his machete, the likelihood that he might spot me sitting there and decide not to hack me to death while he was at it probably wasn't very good at all. The fact that Bob had been kind enough to give me his bedroom to stay in during my visit only seemed to make things worse as I figured that's where Chilango would start the murdering once he got there.

"Yeah, he'd definitely kill you first," Jorge agreed, leaning in once more.

My vacation was officially starting to suck. Making matters worse, we had run out of beer.

"Manuel and I were gonna go to the convenience store if you wanna come," Jorge said. "It's only a few blocks away."

"Weren't you here for that part about how a machete-wielding maniac who'd like nothing more than to chop us all to bits is somewhere out there waiting to do just that?" I replied. "No, thanks."

The attack felt imminent in my mind. After all, once you've decided you're going to julienne a bunch of people with a primitive weapon, I imagine that immediately gets moved to the top of your to-do list.

"Fine," Jorge said. "I guess you could just wait here in the living room by yourself until we get back."

With that, I put on my shoes and followed them out the door. I figured I was probably safer staying with the group. And if I was going to die a savage death, I might as well try to get a couple more beers in me to help cushion the blow.

"This Chilango guy is really starting to piss me off," I said to Jorge and Manuel as we walked, just trying to make conversation.

"Yeah," Jorge said, and shrugged.

As we made our way down the street in the dark, I grew more and more paranoid with each car that passed. And I was disappointed to learn that the convenience store didn't have a license to sell beer on Sunday.

"There's a house down there where we could get some," Jorge said, pointing down an unlit side street.

"What do you mean 'a house'?" I asked.

"There's a guy who sells beer and other stuff on his porch," he explained.

It sounded quaint and all, but ultimately I didn't want more beer that badly. Instead, I grabbed a few delicious tacos from a truck we passed along the way that more than made up for it. And in the end, despite my concerns, we made it back to Bob's house without so much as even our feelings being hurt.

Once back inside, I reluctantly crawled into bed. And even though it was sweltering outside, I decided to shut the window above me. I figured if Chilango decided to come in that way for some reason, the sound of a machete smashing through the windowpane might be enough to wake me and I'd be able to get a decent head start running for my life.

"Good night, Jorge! Good night, Manuel!" I called out in the darkness, like I was on an especially crazy episode of *The Waltons*.

As far as nights where I was convinced some lunatic with a machete might be swinging by to kill everybody go, I somehow managed to get a pretty decent amount of sleep anyway, and was delighted to find, when the roosters woke me up a few hours later, that I didn't have a scratch on me.

Later that morning, I joined Bob in running a few errands and taking in a few more sights around town along the way. Downtown Saltillo is beautiful, with stunning, centuries-old architecture on almost every block. And while I was convinced that one or both of us might take a machete to the face over a measly twenty-five dollars at any second, I was surprised to discover how "in the moment" these circumstances made me feel. It's funny how all the usual stuff like worrying about whether or not you have enough Twitter followers or if your most recent Facebook post has garnered a sufficient number of "likes" starts to seem like much ado about nothing when you think there's even the slightest chance that some guy is waiting around the next corner to lop your head off in one swift motion. I'd yet to find one self-help book that managed to do half as good a job at making me feel quite so present. But maybe I was just trying to look on the bright side.

Grateful to be alive (well, I was, anyway; to his credit, Bob didn't seem as worked up about things), Bob and I headed back to his house that evening, where Manuel, who was now wearing a shirt and seemed way calmer than the last time I'd seen him, was waiting in the driveway again. Once we got back inside, he and Bob chatted with each other in Spanish for a couple minutes, presumably about that whole "Give me my money or I'll kill everybody" thing from the night before, as I stood settled into my by now standard routine of smiling and nodding like I had any clue what was going on.

"What happened with Chilango?" I asked, hoping for some sort of update on any plot developments that might have occurred since I'd last seen Manuel.

"Chilango showed up at Manuel's work today with another thug named La Res,"* Bob explained. "He said if Manuel didn't give him the money, he'd kill everybody tonight."

"And what did Manuel say to that?" I asked. "Just curious."

"He gave him the money," Bob said.

I was relieved to hear it, of course, but given all that stuff from the night before about how Manuel shouldn't pay Chilango, I kept the questions coming.

"Why did he pay him?" I asked.

Bob turned to Manuel and they chatted for a few seconds in Spanish before Bob turned back to me to translate again.

"Manuel said that he was in prison with Chilango, so he knows what he's really like," Bob explained. "And he says that Chilango definitely would have killed us."

"Oh," I replied to Bob before turning to Manuel and saying "*¡Gracias!*"

You should have seen the look on Bob and Manuel's faces when I surprised them with a third Spanish word like that. But that was nothing compared to their reaction when I sprang for beers later.

"What the heck?" I said to Bob as I marched a couple six-

---

* Spanish for "the Beef," it turns out. Not bad.

packs to the checkout counter at the convenience store later on. "A guy saves you from being hacked to death by some jerk with a machete, you pay for the beer that night—that's just manners."

Early the next morning, Bob drove me back to the airport for my flight back to New York City. And while they did end up having some pretty sweet sombreros at the gift shop there, I decided maybe I already had enough to remember my trip by. Instead I gave what few pesos I had left to Bob, shook his hand good-bye, and jumped on the plane home.

When I got back to my apartment that night, I gave my dad a ring to check in.

"I just got back from Mexico," I told him.

"Mexico, huh?" my dad said after a long pause. "I bet your cousin Jean would really like it there."

"Maybe," I replied. "Anyway, it was really nice, but some nut job threatened to kill me and my friends with a machete and the whole trip was almost ruined."

"Jean's a Spanish teacher, you know," my dad continued. "She teaches college kids."

"Yeah, I know, Dad," I said to him. "But what I was saying was—"

"I'm not sure if she's been to Mexico, though," he said, cutting me off.

I tried to bring up the thing about the machete a couple times after that, but eventually there was a knock at his door.

"Well, looks like I gotta go, Dave," my dad said before hanging up. "I'm glad you had a fun trip."

DAVE HILL DOESN'T
LIVE HERE ANYMORE

I'D HAD DRAMATIC VISIONS OF THE DAY WE'D FINALLY say good-bye to what had been the family home for years. My siblings and I would slowly take dusty old picture frames down from the walls and contemplate the blank spaces they'd leave behind before gently packing them away in cardboard boxes. We'd all laugh and maybe even tear up a little bit as we traded fond memories of sending each other to the emergency room, bloodied and unconscious, throughout our formative years and beyond. Leftover bottles of off-brand booze with names like Lewd Stable Boy, Old Puss, and Vaguely Racist Stepdad would be pulled from the kitchen cabinets and emptied directly into our mouths, the toilet, or both. And ideally a mysterious stash of unmarked bills would be discovered underneath the floorboards or in some secret compartment behind a wall and I would stuff it down into my underwear for safekeeping while no one was looking. Finally, we'd gather in the driveway for a reluctant group hug and, who knows, maybe even a sing-along before the house spontaneously burst into flames so high it would require a squadron of helicopters to put them out.

"I'm really gonna miss this place," I'd say, squinting and coughing from all that smoke.

When it actually happened, though, it was surprisingly not much like that at all.

"When are you coming back to Cleveland next?" my sister Libby called to ask me one day about a year after our mother died. "You gotta get all your crap outta here."

It was a call I'd admittedly been dreading since the early nineties, which is when at least half the "crap" Libby was referring to dated back to. Old letters, clothing, baseball cards, even a stack of charcoal sketches from the 100 percent awesome nude-figure drawing course I'd taken right after college when I'd decided I was a sophisticated young man who could make his own goddamn decisions—it was all there, crammed into the attic, the basement, the garage, and just about every other spare crevice in the house as if it were part of the foundation itself. And unlike my siblings, who had all gotten married, bought homes, and went and moved their personal belongings into those homes while they were at it in what I choose to believe was a concerted effort to show off, my plan was to just leave my stuff in the house forever, never to be removed, not even in the event of my untimely death.*

"This is exactly the kind of stuff they're gonna want to have on display at the future Dave Hill museum," I told myself as I imagined throngs of awestruck tourists from around the globe

---

* After all, this baboon heart can't possibly hold up forever.

slowly snaking through my boyhood home turned national land-mark in a single-file line, snapping pictures of each and every mysterious carpet stain I was personally responsible for and doing their damnedest to resist the urge to sneak past the velvet ropes when the heavily armed guards weren't looking so that they might actually touch a pillow or any of the countless other items I'd drooled on a thousand times before with their own bare hands.

"Some say if you listen closely enough late, late at night, you can still hear Dave spending a weirdly long amount of time alone in the upstairs bathroom," the tour guides would be forced to say over and over again to the delight and amazement of every man, woman, and child in attendance. It was going to be so, so great. For everybody.

Unfortunately, however, Libby had a different vision. As the only sibling still living in Cleveland, she'd been saddled with the chore of helping my dad get the house ready to be put on the mar-ket. And a big part of that, she repeatedly and annoyingly ex-plained, had to do with my getting my aforementioned crap the hell out of there.

"Mice have started to eat through all of your stuff in the ga-rage, you know," Libby mentioned in an attempt to get me to focus. "It's pretty gross, actually."

"Not gross enough to get me to do anything about it," I re-plied.

On the surface, I guess it was just plain old laziness combined with the hassle of figuring out where in my relatively tiny New York City apartment I might possibly find space for any more stuff that had me putting it off for so long. But deep down inside

I knew that what I was probably having a tougher time with was the dread of officially saying good-bye to my youth and acknowledging that I was a grown-ass man who could literally never go home again without someone calling the cops once my dad had sold the place. After all, this was the place my parents had first moved into with my two older sisters in the late sixties after they'd outgrown apartment living, the place where my dad had tried and failed to grow a thick and lustrous lawn each and every summer for over forty years, the place where my mom's signature slightly too dry chicken breasts had been met with weary resignation a thousand times before, the place where bill collectors called looking for me well into my thirties, and—perhaps most important—the place I'd always figured that if all else failed I could maybe come back to and crash for a while as I plotted my "next move."

But suddenly that was all about to change. With my mother gone, my dad had quickly grown tired of living in the house all by himself. The loneliness was a given, but all sorts of other problems had begun to crop up, too. For example, with no one else in the place with him, it could take days or even weeks for him to find a set of car keys, a tuna sandwich, or whatever else he might have absentmindedly set down somewhere as he went about his day.

"It's just too big for one person anymore," my dad explained, presumably still racking his brain over where the hell that sandwich might have gotten off to. "It's awful quiet, too."

It's not like I disagreed with him. As soon as my mom died, the house felt instantly cavernous to me, like one of those abandoned old houses Shaggy, Velma, Daphne, and that dick in the

ascot would somehow stumble upon in at least every other episode of *Scooby-Doo*. And suddenly every room felt the same. The
kitchen, the dining room, the living room, and the family room,
each with its own specific purpose and unspoken set of rules
we'd been trained to at least occasionally follow since we were
kids—it just felt like an endless maze, vaguely familiar at best.
It was as if the circus had left town and, like it or not, it was now
time to go.

Despite all of this, however, I somehow counted on never having to actually remove any of my stuff from the place. And there
was a lot of it. For example, sometime during my college years,
my friend Tony and I, like so many young men with a penchant
for crafts before us, had become so transfixed by an episode of
The New Yankee Workshop on which Norm Abram made something called an Adirondack chair out of ordinary scraps of wood
that we decided to build our very own, far crappier version right
in the middle of my family's driveway the very next day, while
my parents were conveniently out of town. The chair only kinda,
sorta was completed and only kinda, sorta resembled the flawless
perch Norm had whipped up without even really needing to put
on his safety goggles,* and I pushed it into a dusty corner of the
garage that very same day, where it remained untouched, like
some sad modern sculpture, never to be sat in even once for nearly
two decades, as it served alternately as something to lean lawn-
care equipment against and as a shelter of sorts for whatever
small woodland creatures might happen to wander into the ga-

---

* Please note that Norm did, in fact, put his safety goggles on, though. We can
all totally learn from his example.

rage on days when someone had accidentally left the door wide open (which is to say most days).

"You still want that Adirondack chair?" my dad would call to ask me at least once a year. "It's taking up half the garage."

"What Adirondack chair?" I'd reply.

"The one you and Tony built that one weekend when your mother and I went out of town in the nineties," my dad would explain.

"Okay, now what garage?" I'd then ask before changing the topic altogether. It was great.

Eventually he'd forget about it until the following fall, when he happened to be looking for a rake or something, stumble upon the Adirondack chair all over again, and think, "That son of a bitch" while presumably shaking his fist in the air.

Now, suddenly, after more than four decades of our family calling the place home, the Adirondack chair, the used, one-piece clown costume that had been so heavily discounted only an idiot would have passed it up, the belt sander I'd borrowed from my friend Phil and decided to just hang on to after his indictment, and everything else I'd ever dragged into the house all had to go.

"Why do you even have this stuff in the first place?" Libby asked, weirdly frustrated.

"I guess I just appreciate the finer things," I explained.

Of course, all the stuff in the house that wasn't mine had to go, too. My dad called dibs on a few things, but my siblings—the ones with the spouses and houses I was talking about earlier— took care of most of the bigger items my dad didn't want, like old armchairs, dinner platters suitable for serving hams and other large shanks of meat, antique mirrors, and other stuff people with property and full lives tend to gravitate toward. But, given the fact that I barely had room for an extra coaster in my apartment, the only thing I took that wasn't mine to begin with was my mother's old ice skates, partly for the memory but also because I didn't want them getting into the wrong hands. As for the Adirondack chair, I told my dad he could just throw it in the trash, something that, after letting it take up space in the garage all those years for apparently no reason whatsoever, he handled with admirable grace.

Thanks to some savvy call screening on my part, I managed to get Libby to deal with almost everything else. When she finally managed to corner me long enough to go through whatever was left during one of my visits home, it had already been whittled down to just five or six boxes she'd placed out in the garage on a shelf only a really special mouse could possibly reach. I then reluctantly pared those boxes down to just three or four boxes, which, in turn, I conveniently "forgot" to take back to New York. I'm not bragging or anything, but ultimately Libby was forced to store them in her basement before eventually shipping them to me without warning. As soon as they arrived, I just shoved them under the bed along with some instructions I'd typed up for those museum people I remained certain would show up one day.

But as much as a complete pain in the butt it was to get all my stuff out of the house (well, for Libby, anyway), there ended up not being that much of a hurry to get it done, after all, as—even with its rich history of being the house where I had lived throughout my youth and then again to celebrate my thirtieth birthday for a couple years after that—somehow no one seemed all that interested in looking at the place. Once prime suburban Cleveland real estate, the neighborhood I'd grown up in was now considered "a little too close to the city"* and "not modern enough," according to the real estate agent my dad and Libby had brought in to unload our "quaint four-bedroom" that was "close to all the shops" and "great for a young family or Boo Radley type looking for a fresh start."

"Most prospective Cleveland homeowners tend to prefer the brand-new homes being built in towns farther away from the city," she explained while furrowing her brow in a manner that suggested sympathy of some sort.

It turned out the houses she was referring to were located in areas we'd known in simpler times as "the woods." Meanwhile, it seemed that most of the deer that had been living in those woods before all those new houses were built had decided to come hang out at my dad's place. Suddenly it was pretty much business as usual to see three or four of them at a time, eating my dad's bushes for lunch and sunning themselves in his backyard, mere feet from his Barcalounger, like they were on some sort of weird deer spring break.

"I bet I can take a bigger dump in Dave's dad's backyard than the rest of you assholes," I imagined them saying to one another in the secret deer language I am confident exists.

My dad got used to the deer pretty quickly. But since I'd never seen a beast more exotic than a hamster on our block the whole time I'd ever lived there, it took me a while to adjust to them on my visits home.

---

* Real estate–speak for "You didn't hear it from me, but someone saw a black guy driving down the street."

"Holy shit!" I accidentally blurted at the sight of an eight-point buck standing in our driveway and apparently not being even the least bit concerned that my dad and I were trying to leave for the Sunglass Hut.

"Watch your language or we're going right back in the house," my dad grunted at me. But even that wouldn't get the buck to budge. They can be real dicks sometimes.

Eventually, the real estate agent suggested that perhaps the circa 1969 wallpaper and the thick, green wall-to-wall carpet in the house might also be scaring off prospective buyers, and that if every trace of our family's existence—mine especially, it seemed implied—was wiped from its floors, walls, and even ceilings while we were at it, the house might sell faster and for more money.

"You want to come home one week and do some painting and stuff?" Libby asked me. "We have to pay someone to do it, so it might as well be you."

"What's that?" I asked. "The reception isn't so good where I am right now. You still there? Libby?"

Way back in the nineties, I used to earn a few extra bucks slapping a few coats of paint on the walls of suburban Cleveland homeowners with especially low standards. I was determined to keep those days behind me, though, so I declined my sister's offer to come out of retirement.

Besides, I knew how these things usually went—one minute you're painting the living room, the next you're regrouting the bathroom tile, the next you're going through all that crap of yours in cardboard boxes up in the attic.

"No, thanks," I thought. "I could die up there."

Stymied, my sister arranged for some creepy yet well-meaning loner with a van to come remove the wallpaper and carpet, paint the walls, and stain the floors. When he was all done, Libby sent me an e-mail that contained photos of a house, with no explanation.

"Whose house is this?" I asked obliviously.

"Ours," she replied.

"Wow," I wrote back. The place was unrecognizable. Suddenly it looked ridiculously spacious and charming, like it might even smell of freshly baked pies that had been effortlessly whipped up by an attractive young mother who had no trouble whatsoever losing the extra weight after her pregnancy. I almost thought about putting an offer in on the place myself.

Even with the face-lift, though, the real estate agent somehow still couldn't unload the place. So, after the house had been on the market for over a year without a single offer being made, my dad decided to just go ahead and move out anyway, decamping for the retirement community a few towns over, not far from where those deer probably used to live.

But even my dad's moving out wasn't enough to get me to move on from the family home myself. Both he and Libby were now living in suburbs that might as well have been in Canada, as far as I was concerned, so rather than trying to navigate the roads near either of their homes and risk taking out a mailbox or a jogging club or something, I decided it was easier to return to the address I already had memorized.

"There's a set of keys in the garage and an air mattress upstairs," Libby told me in advance of my next trip back home.

"Sounds cozy," I told her. "Can't wait."

I flew into Cleveland around ten o'clock on a Friday night and drove straight to the house from the airport in my rental car. It wasn't until I was actually pulling into the driveway that I suddenly remembered that no one in my family even lived there anymore, that it was just an empty house now only vaguely resembling the one I'd grown up in. It was so unsettling at first that part of me considered just asking the next-door neighbors if I might crash at their place instead. But not wanting to deal with their telling me what I could and couldn't have in their fridge or any of that nonsense, I forged ahead and fetched the keys from the garage.

As I let myself in through the side door, I remembered how our old dog Chloe would rush to the door to either greet or growl at anyone who entered, depending on her mood and on whether or not she felt that person had wronged her at any point over the years. And I remembered how my dad would usually yell, "That you, Dave?" from some corner of the house before I'd even taken my shoes off. And how my mom would suddenly appear in the kitchen doorway, asking me how my day or night was and whether or not I'd brought home ice cream or some other snack that we'd quickly devour on the spot before anyone else in the house was even aware of its existence. Now it was impossibly quiet except for the sound of my own footsteps.

As strange as the house felt, though, I found that as long as I kept most of the lights off and blurred my eyes a bit as I walked upstairs, it was easy enough to at least momentarily pretend that everything was totally normal and all of our stuff wasn't missing.

Once I found the air mattress Libby had set up for me, I quickly drifted off to sleep, just as I'd done in that house thousands of times before. A couple hours later, though, I was awoken by some college students, who'd been renting a house on the block, as they pounded beers and chatted in their driveway the way that young people who think they're going to live forever are wont to do. It didn't bother me much, but when I thought about the fact that they might also be waking up my old neighbors, the people I'd known since I was a little kid, the people who'd been forced to put up with my own bullshit for decades, I suddenly felt I owed it to all of them to head outside and hand these college kids a verbal beat-down. So I sat up on the air mattress and began pulling on my pants and shoes with purpose. But then I suddenly had a powerful vision of a bunch of drunken college kids in backward baseball caps, flip-flops, and cargo shorts severely outnumbering me as they whipped me around like a rag doll in my own backyard, cackling as they called me names like "old bitch," "dicklips," and "fucking fuckface," and I reverted to a slightly less heroic plan B.

"Um, yeah," I said to the grumpy officer who answered the phone at the police department down the street moments later. "There's some college kids next door to my house and they're talking really loudly and disturbing me and some other people, I bet, and it's causing me great difficulty in sleeping and . . ."

"All right," the officer said, cutting me off. "I'll make a note of it."

"Oh, and I'm pretty sure they're drinking beer," I added. "Lots and lots of beer. Probably illegally! I can hear the bottles and cans and everything. It's, it's *awful!*"

"Would you like to file a complaint?" the officer asked.

"No," I said, "I was wondering if you could maybe go over there and ask them to stop, please."

"Okay," the officer grunted back at me. "We'll send a car over."

I was about to tell the officer how normally I would have just gone over to the house and kicked everybody's asses all over the place myself and probably taken whatever was left of their beer while I was at it, but it was late and I was too tired to beat the crap out of a bunch of college kids single-handedly before taking their beer and also making out with their girlfriends, now that I think about it, even though I probably totally could have if I felt like it, but he hung up on me before I had the chance.

"Th-thank you," I said to the dial tone before hanging up myself.

Still wired from not actually leaving the house to hand out my own swift brand of justice to those college kids, I headed downstairs to the kitchen to calm my nerves with one of the beers from the six-pack I had bought on the way back to the house because I am a grown man and my dad or anyone else can't say shit about it.

As I stood there sipping my beer and staring out the kitchen window at the backyard, still lit up by the garage light I'd forgotten to turn off, I thought back to the countless hours I used to spend sitting out there on our long-gone swing set. Or practicing my slap shot to the delight and amazement of an imaginary hockey arena full of people watching my every dazzling move. Or lying in the grass, daydreaming about becoming the new fifth member of Kiss or maybe someday actually kissing a girl. Then suddenly my mind drifted to a story I'd heard once about a family that had packed up and moved to a new home several miles away. Somewhere along the line, they ended up losing their dog, only to find him a couple days later, back at the old house, just sitting there at the side door, presumably wondering what the hell happened.

And it was at that moment that I realized that dog was me.

A BUSTLE IN
MY HEDGEROW

IT'S A POPULAR OPINION AMONG FANS OF ROCK MUSIC that the greatest rock song of all time is "Stairway to Heaven" by Led Zeppelin. And there's a reason for it, too—the greatest rock song of all time is "Stairway to Heaven" by Led Zeppelin. Or at least that's what the thirteen-year-old me was pretty convinced of when I started to take guitar lessons during the summer before eighth grade. And to be fair, a lot of other thirteen-year-old boys, especially those learning to play guitar, were convinced of the same thing. The difference, however, was that I was determined, determined to rock, determined to shred, determined to learn "Stairway to Heaven" so well that gnomes, at least a couple of the ancients, and maybe even a mysterious woman dressed head to toe in lace and easily given to scampering about would suddenly appear every time I played it, dammit.

Of course, these were simpler times, and the ability to just hop online or even flip through a magazine and find "Stairway to

Heaven" all figured out for you already and written in tablature, a notation that assured guitar players everywhere that they'd never have to actually learn what music notes and other nerdy musical stuff were, wasn't yet a regular thing. And what with "Stairway" being a song handed down from the fucking gods (i.e., Led Zeppelin) and all, it seemed brazen to even think about trying to play it by ear, the way I had done with Deep Purple's "Smoke on the Water"* and any number of other stone-cold jams, sitting there in my underwear on the edge of my bed, guitar in hand as I slowly hammered out the melody like a caveman discovering fire. So I had no choice but to learn how to play "Stairway to Heaven" the old-fashioned way: by sitting down in front of some sheet music, squinting, and picking along until eventually I managed to get my guitar to make a sound somewhere in the ballpark of what Jimmy Page had in mind when he originally composed it, presumably by torchlight.

My guitar teacher at the time was a guy named Joe from the next town over. I rode my sister Libby's ten-speed to his house, clumsily steering with one hand and carrying my guitar in its beat-up hard case with the other, determined to be schooled like a mofo each week in the ways of rock while hoping nobody would see me riding a girl's bike, something that could set me back

---

* I realize there is a slight implication here that Ritchie Blackmore and the rest of the original lineup of Deep Purple are not also gods. They are. Even so, they couldn't beat Led Zeppelin in a rock fight in a million, trillion years, and if anyone disagrees with me on this, just name the Burger King parking lot you would like to meet up in to discuss this matter further and I will be there with a six-pack and my fists.

weeks in eighth-grade social circles. Joe had a sunburst Gibson Les Paul guitar just like Jimmy Page and, in anticipation of young bucks like me who wanted to learn the greatest rock song of all time, had already transcribed "Stairway to Heaven" onto sheet music by hand like a Burgundian monk or something. When I asked him if I, this scrappy young kid from the next town over, could learn it, he looked at me skeptically, maybe even a bit pitifully, for a moment before finally snuffing out his Marlboro Red and speaking.

"You really think you can handle it?" Joe asked, scratching his head in a manner that suggested he totally didn't think I could.

"You really think you can handle me walking in here next week and melting your fucking face right off by playing 'Stairway to Heaven' note for note mere feet from where you and your loved ones sleep every night?" I wanted to ask him back before quietly mumbling "Yes" instead.

Generally speaking, I wasn't big on confidence at the time. But for some reason I was still pretty sure Jimmy Page and Robert Plant had written "Stairway to Heaven" entirely with the idea that a young Dave Hill, who lived just a few thousand miles away from them, across the Atlantic in Cleveland, would eventually do their masterpiece justice by locking himself in his bedroom for as long as it took to learn every note of it on his guitar in accordance with a prophecy there was no way in hell anyone else in suburban Cleveland could even begin to understand. When Joe reluctantly handed me the sheet music, I folded it up and shoved it in my pants like I'd just been given a secret treasure map, a secret treasure map of rock, which was awesome.

"Thanks, Joe," I told him before marching out his front door. "You won't regret this."

"We'll see," Joe chuckled on his front porch, lighting up another smoke while I pedaled off into the summer sun as if my life had officially just begun.

As it turned out, it took exactly one week for me to learn "Stairway to Heaven," during which I ate little, slept even less, and pretty much dispensed with bathing altogether. When I walked into Joe's living room with my ax at my side for my next lesson, he appeared mildly concerned for my health. In reality, however, it was his own health he should have been worried about, because little did he know I was about to completely blow his mind right out of his skull and all over his living room wall probably by playing all seven minutes and fifty-eight seconds of "Stairway to Heaven" without even stopping to see if he still had a pulse. I probably should have had him sign a waiver.

I picked up my guitar and Joe leaned back in his chair, smirking ever so slightly and likely assuming he would have to interrupt me for screwing up before I even got through the intro.

"All right," Joe said. "Let's hear what you got."

With that I began plucking those first few notes familiar to anyone who has ever worked in a guitar store anywhere ever. My playing was tentative at first, but once I got to the part where Robert Plant would normally come in, I no longer felt alone and began to relax and settle into the song a bit more comfortably, almost like Satan himself had risen up from Joe's shag carpet and placed one of his creepy red hands on my shoulder for rock guidance or something. And by the time I launched into the second verse, I'm pretty sure Joe must have thought I was the coolest thirteen-year-old he had hung out with in his living room in his entire life.

During the part at the end where Robert Plant sings, ". . . and she's buying a stairway to heaven" for the last time, Joe and I both paused momentarily to stare off into the distance together as if to glimpse a comet tail before I came back in with the final notes to drive that bitch home for good.

"I gotta admit," Joe said once I finally finished, "I'm pretty impressed."

"Yeah, Joe," I thought, briefly considering spitting on the carpet for emphasis before thinking better of it. "I bet you are."

We continued the lesson after that, but it was admittedly hard to focus, because when you're thirteen and you've just managed to play the greatest rock song of all time from start to finish, it's hard to imagine there's much else left to accomplish in life, even on the guitar. Twenty minutes later, I was out the door, riding home on my sister's ten-speed and feeling like a man.

As fate would have it, a few weeks later there was a talent show at school and I talked some of the other musicians in the eighth grade into playing "Stairway to Heaven" with me onstage. My friend Riley owned a drum set and my friend Kevin had agreed to sing and play guitar along with me, even though— as far as "Stairway to Heaven" was concerned, anyway—he couldn't really do either. It didn't matter, though, as I was confident I could handle most of the heavy lifting, and as long as Kevin managed not to turn his amp up too loud, we'd be fine. The one thing missing, though, was the outro guitar solo, the greatest guitar solo of all time* that just so happened to be a part of the greatest rock song of all time. I knew how to play the rest of the song, of course, but the solo was still very much out of my grasp.

"Those are some pretty tricky licks," Joe explained to me at my next lesson after I pleaded with him to show me how it was done. "It's not just about the notes—it's gotta feel right, too."

Looking back on it, I realize Joe was sugarcoating things. The reality was and still is that in order to properly play the solo to "Stairway to Heaven," you have to be able to put a little bit of sex into it or at least have already gone through most of puberty. Some might argue you even have to come to some sort of agreement or another with the devil while you're at it, too. That is, if you really want to nail it anyway. Regardless, when I was thirteen and still living with my parents in the suburbs, all three of those things were still quite a ways off. Still, I was determined, so when I got home from Joe's house that night and then every night after that until the day of the talent show, I struggled to learn that solo note for note, puberty, sex, and Beelzebub be damned.

By the time the talent show finally rolled around, I could play the first few notes of the solo fairly convincingly, at least for a

---

* In case you're interested, while I still think the guitar solo to "Stairway to Heaven" is totally sweet and definitely still *one* of the greatest guitar solos of all time, as of this writing, I tend to think Ron Wood's solo on "Maggie May" by Rod Stewart is actually *the* greatest guitar solo of all time. It's perfect. Congrats, Ron—you really hit it out of the park with that one. Your other band is good, too.

virgin who hadn't already gone to the dark side anyway. But after those first few notes, things kind of trailed off and I was forced to just play the rhythm guitar like I did at Joe's house that day. And when Kevin, Riley, and I finally took the stage at the talent show, I was too nervous to even try playing any of the solo at all. Instead, I just bashed away on the outro chords until one of the nuns gave us the wave that it was time to wrap things up so that one of our classmates could do some bullshit jazz tap dancing routine or whatever. And as for Kevin, he either lost his nerve to sing or maybe never bothered to learn the words to the song in the first place, so it ended up being an entirely instrumental version of "Stairway to Heaven" in the end, which turned out to be fine, since we didn't have a microphone for him to sing into anyway.

"That was pretty good," my friend John told me once we finished. "I mean, you know, all things considered."

Under any other circumstances, I might have just taken the compliment. But as far as I was concerned, "pretty good" wasn't nearly good enough in this case. I was supposed to rip a sweet guitar solo at the end of "Stairway to Heaven" in front of my whole class and I totally blew it. All these years later, it still gets to me a little bit whenever I think about it or run into one of the girls from my class at the grocery store when I'm home visiting my dad or something.

"How are you doing, Dave?" they ask me. But I swear they're mostly wondering whether or not I can play the solo to "Stairway to Heaven" yet.

As you can probably imagine, I sit here today, a man fully

capable of ripping the solo to "Stairway to Heaven" without even really trying. And I didn't even have to get Satan involved to do it—mostly I just practiced a lot. I mean, I can't play it quite like Jimmy Page, but I'd like to think he'd approve.

"That's some pretty great playing, Dave," I imagine Jimmy telling me. "In some ways I like it better than my own version." Then we'd just sit there having tea and looking at his knife collection or something in his English mansion while some hot chick stands in the corner playing a theremin.

Backing things up a bit, it's worth noting at this point that my appreciation of the magic and majesty of "Stairway to Heaven" and Led Zeppelin in general began with my father, who brought home a copy of *Led Zeppelin IV* at a time when pop, jazz, and classical music were about all I'd ever heard playing in our house. In fact, it's the only rock record I remember him ever buying. Not long ago, he brought it up again.

"I was listening to Led Zeppelin the other day," he told me. "That 'Stairway to Heaven' is really something."

"Duh," I thought before telling him that thing about how it's the greatest rock song of all time.

"Probably," he said. "But I still think they don't attack the ending hard enough."

"Really?" I asked.

"Yeah," he said. "I just think it could have been even bigger somehow."

It takes a lot of nerve to go criticizing the ending to the greatest rock song of all time from out of nowhere like that, but I guess when you're eighty-two you can say crazy stuff like that and get away with it.

Recently, I visited my dad and found that he had bought the sheet music to "Stairway to Heaven."

"I thought it might sound nice on piano," he explained.

I had never heard the song on piano before, so I asked him to go ahead and play it for me.

"I can only play the first few bars so far," he told me, "but I'll give it a shot."

Then he sat down at the old upright piano in his apartment and began to hammer out the familiar, even life-changing melody. I have to admit, it was pretty awesome, partly because it was "Stairway to Heaven," but also because an eighty-two-year-old man sitting down and playing it on the piano is just something you don't really see coming, even when he tells you that's exactly what he's going to do.

As my dad sat there playing, I had an idea.

"Hey, Dad," I said, interrupting him at the top of the second verse, "when you learn the rest of it, do you think I could maybe sit in on guitar and play the solo at the end of the song along with you?" I figured it could be my way of making things right after all these years.

"I guess that would be fine," he replied after seemingly thinking about it for a second.

"Cool." I nodded. "Really cool."

I called my dad a few days ago to see how things were coming along. He said he still had a ways to go before he could play the whole song, which I admittedly found a bit annoying.

"What the hell else does an eighty-two-year-old man have to

do all day except learn 'Stairway to Heaven' on piano so that his kid can come over and rip a face-melting solo guitar all over it?" I thought.

Even so, I decided not to ride him too hard about it. The important thing is that once he finally gets there, I'll be ready, really, *really* ready.

And I am going to completely blow his fucking mind.

ROLLING THUNDER

ONE OF THE HARDEST REALIZATIONS I'VE COME TO in life aside from the fact that I have combination skin is that I'm a lot like my parents. It's not because I have anything against them. In fact, as far as having parents goes, I totally lucked out. It's just that while growing up—like a lot of children, I'm guessing—I preferred to think of myself as unique, my own person, a golden child with traits and qualities all my own no matter what it said on my birth certificate, almost as if I had just been found inside a hollow tree in the woods one day rather than actually being the product of my parents doing the unthinkable. But slowly, over time, I couldn't help but notice, for example, that I can lose a set of house keys at least as quickly as my mother used to and look pretty much like her in male drag while doing it. Or that my father and I have almost identical patches of body hair and are both so weirdly bad at shooting free throws in basketball that it should probably be considered a medical disability.

But unfortunately it doesn't end there. I, like my father, snore like a damn bear. And not just any bear, either—I'm talking about a bear with a deviated septum, a touch of black lung, and at least a couple gallons of scotch coursing through its veins at all times. Please note that I am describing a fictional bear here and am in no way suggesting that my dad is or has ever been a scotch man. My point is simply that the snoring is really, really bad.

The fact that my dad snored was no secret—it couldn't be— but on a good night he could practically shake the roof loose. As a kid, I just dismissed it as "something dads do." Still, I never thought it would happen to me, a guy who had his whole breathing life ahead of him. Then one day, I found out the hard way.

"Why am I covered in old shoes and empty beer cans?" I asked my buddies after waking up hungover and confused in some strange living room during my junior year in college on what some might call a "road trip."

"We were trying to get you to stop snoring," my friend Pete explained. "It was awful."

"What are you talking about?" I asked. "I don't snore."

"You snore worse than anyone I've ever heard in my whole life," my other buddy Tim countered, as if I'd gone ahead and taken a crap on the rug while I was at it.

It was all downhill from there. From that day forward, all I ever heard from anyone forced to share sleeping quarters with me—whether their experience had been the by-product of some shared desire to give the finger to maximum-occupancy rules at Best Western or something else entirely—was that my snoring was "awful," "the worst," and that it "sounded like I was definitely, definitely going to die." Some people—assholes, I call them—even seemed convinced my snoring was something I could easily control and that I was actually doing it on purpose, presumably just to be a prick.

"Can you *please* stop doing that?" they'd ask, bleary-eyed after a sleepless night spent trying to block out my stentorian snoring. "It's really inconsiderate."

Anyway, somewhere around this time, my mother, finally fed up with my dad's snoring after twenty-five years or so of sleepless nights, began banishing him to my room to crash in my brother Bob's old bed on nights when my dad was really taking things to the next level.

"I can't sleep," I'd complain to my mom the next morning. "Dad's snoring is horrible."

"*My* snoring's horrible?" he'd say. "*Yours* is even worse."

A father and son suddenly turned against each other—it was the stuff of Greek tragedy.

Eventually, my dad decided to get the medical community involved, who in turn quickly determined he had sleep apnea, the not-so-silent killer. As you may already know, sleep apnea is a fancy way of saying a person momentarily stops breathing in his sleep, causing a buildup of carbon dioxide in the bloodstream, which in turn causes the person to wake up so that he can start taking in oxygen again. As if that's not annoying enough, it's usually accompanied by the thunderous snoring my dad and I had both gained a rep for around town. And in the most extreme cases, it can even cause death, which is negative any way you slice it but still something I'm sure at least a few people forced to share a room with me secretly hoped for.

To treat my dad's sleep apnea, doctors suggested he start

using a contraption called a CPAP (or "continuous positive airway pressure" for people who hate abbreviations) machine at night that would stop his snoring/keep him breathing/make it so he wouldn't die in his sleep, something that makes for an awkward breakfast in the majority of cases. The CPAP machine was about the size of a toaster, and as soon as my dad began using it, a quiet, mechanical hum could be heard emanating from my parents' room in place of his abominable snoring, kind of like John Travolta in the hit movie *The Boy in the Plastic Bubble*, a film we still talk about to this day.

As for me, I just kept on snoring like a mofo. Somewhere along the way, I read that snoring was actually something humans and other living things developed over time as a defense mechanism, sort of a way of telling would-be predators or anyone else thinking about waking them up and possibly futzing with their genitals* that they should seriously think twice about it or they might be mauled or at the very least get called names as a result of their intrusion. I'm not sure if snoring had that effect in my case, but once I got really good at it, it did, for example, make it so that no one ever wanted to share a room at the Best Western or anywhere else with me again.

"You're welcome to share a room with me," I'd offer a would-be roommate, "but I should warn you—you won't sleep a wink."

Now that I'm rereading it, I guess it sounded kind of creepy at first, like I might force them to participate in diabolical medical experiments involving latex, goggles, and rusty old clamps I had

---

* A very popular reason for waking someone up, statistically speaking anyway.

come up with in my spare time, or maybe even gently stroke their hair while humming traditional folk melodies for hours at a time. But after I got around to explaining the whole snoring thing, I'd usually end up getting my own room, after all. And on the rare occasions that I didn't, I'd usually wake up covered in old shoes and empty beer cans like that time back in college.

But the jig was finally up after my sister Miriam brought her then-boyfriend/now-husband, Nick, home to meet my parents* one weekend. Because of Jesus† and also because we didn't have a spare room, Nick was forced to sleep in my sister Katy's old room with me and was completely horrified.

"I've never heard anything quite like it in my entire life," Nick groaned at the breakfast table the next morning. "I thought he might die right then and there."

Miriam seemed momentarily hopeful after that last part. But regardless, as is often the case when a non–family member complains about something, my snoring suddenly became a serious issue as far as the rest of my family was concerned.

"You really should get that checked out," Miriam urged, presumably having rethunk things.

"Yeah, you might have sleep apnea," my dad agreed, seemingly a little too pumped that I might share his affliction. "I have it, so odds are good you have it, too—that's just genetics."

---

* And, by default, me, as I was visiting that weekend, too.

† I.e., religious reasons. My parents didn't want my sister and her boyfriend sharing a room before marriage. We're Irish Catholic—you're gonna get that every now and again.

It was kind of annoying, especially since I was just trying to get through my cereal without incident, but in the end I agreed to get it checked out. So when I got back to New York, I signed up for something called a sleep study, where a team of people with blank stares and lab coats ask you to slip into a hospital gown, hook you up to a bunch of wires, point a camera at your bed, and tell you to go to sleep in a strange, windowless room three hours before your normal bedtime, like nothing weird is happening at all.

"Don't mind us," one of the lab coat people told me before turning off the lights in the windowless room I had been assigned to. "We'll just be watching you sleep on a monitor in the next room."

"Thank you?" I replied.

It felt like a lot of pressure. And it wasn't because of the whole snoring thing, either. I was more worried about all the other stuff I tend to do in my sleep—like telling my deepest darkest secrets, mumbling show tunes I don't have the range for, or even yanking my boxers down to my ankles with a frequency gentlemen don't discuss. Even so, I somehow managed to conk out for the night just a few minutes after lights-out. It's a wonder what a bed with actual sheets and blankets and pillowcases and a frame to boot will do for you sometimes. And even with all the wires, the camera, and the team of determined weirdos all watching me on a monitor in some nearby room, I managed to sleep almost as much as I usually did in my own bed.

"Time to wake up," a mysterious voice notified me through a speaker next to my bed at a ghastly six thirty the next morning, a time when only surgeons, paperboys, and go-go dancers on self-destruct tend to be awake. "That concludes your sleep study."

As soon as I heard it, I immediately became self-conscious again and started to wonder exactly what disturbing stuff I might have gotten up to during the night in my sleep. Then I pulled my clothes on and walked over to the room where, speaking of disturbing, all the people in the lab coats sat with looks on their faces that suggested equal amounts of judgment and concern.

"You definitely have sleep apnea," one of them, presumably the leader, told me, like she'd just won a bet and all her coworkers better start reaching for their wallets posthaste or they would no longer be eligible for the company-wide drawing to win a trip to Cancun. "We recorded over one hundred fifty instances where you woke up and/or stopped breathing in your sleep last night."

It felt like some kind of record and, despite the seemingly bad news, it was still hard not to be a little bit proud of that statistic, at least for a few seconds anyway.

As I walked out of the sleep study building and into the cold morning a few minutes later, I thought to call my dad and give him the news, but I didn't want to give him the satisfaction just yet. Instead, I agreed to return to the sleep study place the following week so they could sit in their little room like a bunch of snoring fetishists and watch me sleep again. This time around, though, I would be hooked up to a machine not unlike the one my dad by now talked about so much, you'd swear he'd landed an endorsement deal.

"Good night," a woman in a lab coat and glasses said to me as she finished strapping what looked like a protective cup* attached to a hose of some sort to my face.

"Good night," I mumbled back to her, trying to pretend this was completely normal and I did shit like this all the time.

"We'll see you in the morning," she said with a finality that suggested that might not be the case at all, before heading for the door.

Regardless, the game had suddenly changed. With this contraption strapped to my face, I could no longer just drift off to some semblance of sleep that would apparently be interrupted a whopping 150 times without my somehow even noticing. Instead, a blast of damp air was being pumped through my nostrils, somehow forcing my mouth shut while it was at it, and making it so that whatever all the loose flesh inside my head† is called could no longer flap around and make it so that my now brother-in-law‡ Nick was afraid he was going to wake up with a body on his hands and, as a result, would no longer be welcome to "help himself to whatever he'd like in the fridge," as my mother had told him upon first meeting. Likewise, I was now actually breathing as I fell asleep, something I was by this point in my life mostly unfamiliar with. In short, it took some getting used to.

---

* You know, the kind a man wears before taking part in certain athletics, to make sure there will one day be children to take care of him as he waits for death.

† Actually it's called the uvula, but I'm not comfortable admitting I have one of those just yet.

‡ Speaking of which, Nick, I realize I still owe you and Miriam a wedding gift. Sorry about that. I promise I haven't forgotten. Also, happy tenth anniversary!

"Good morning," the mysterious voice from before said to me again at six thirty the next morning. "Time to wake up."

I had somehow forgotten about all the complex machinery that had been strapped to my head the night before and even the strange room I had slept in, too, so once I fully regained consciousness, I worried for a second that I had been in a car wreck or maybe gotten involved with a woman who liked to get weird. But then I remembered how I had actually paid to have somebody do this to me.

"You responded very well to the sleep machine," one of the lab coat people told me back in his lair after I'd gotten dressed and fixed my hair.

It sounded like something out of an especially creepy sci-fi movie. But I guess the point was the machine got me to finally stop snoring, so a few days later, I went ahead and let some guy into my apartment to show me how to use the new CPAP machine the people in the lab coats insisted I get whether my insurance would cover it or not. He had a decidedly non-medical way about him, almost like he could have just as easily been a door-to-door vaccuum cleaner salesman, which, the more I think about it, I guess he kind of was.

"You put it on like this," the guy said, strapping the contraption to my face like they had done back at the sleep study place. He spoke in a disinterested manner that suggested he didn't want to be sitting in my apartment telling me this stuff any more than I wanted him to be, that maybe just as soon as he got out of there, he'd douse his carload of CPAP machines with gasoline, toss a match on them, and say good-bye to the CPAP game once and for all. The very idea of it kind of made me like the guy. Who knows? Maybe under different circumstances we could have become good friends, two guys who walk the earth not giving a rat's ass about anything, especially unobstructed breathing. But I guess it just wasn't meant to be.

"Thanks," I told him, showing him the door a few minutes later after he barely got through his presentation. "I had a nice time."

That night I reluctantly took my new CPAP machine for its maiden voyage. Somehow hooking myself up to this weird machine in my own bedroom felt even more violating, like something out of a deleted scene from *A Clockwork Orange* or perhaps the work of some prankster with way too much time on his hands. And each time I woke up in the middle of the night, I had to remind myself what it was and why it was strapped to my face like that and that it wasn't all part of some sick pastime or another I'd recently taken a shine to.

On the medical side of things, however, I assumed the machine succeeded in stopping my snoring and also helping me to achieve a better night's sleep, but it was really hard to tell since, you know, I was asleep and all. For what it's worth, I did notice it had the interesting side effect of making all my dreams and even nightmares somehow more pleasant. For example, during my pre–CPAP machine nights, if I'd had a dream in which, for example, some madman who just so happened to look just like my high school gym teacher in a mascot uniform was chasing me around Bed Bath & Beyond with a butcher knife, I'd wake up in a cold sweat, worried the madman was still waiting to slash my throat and I'd never find the right duvet cover just as soon as I drifted off to sleep again. But with the CPAP machine hooked up to my face, suddenly that scenario would just seem like a dream about a really fun game I was playing. And I would find the perfect duvet cover every single time! It was kind of awesome. Who knows—maybe I was getting too much oxygen.

Assorted side effects aside, the CPAP machine did make it awkward to sleep in the same room with anyone. In fact, guaranteed celibacy is probably the biggest side effect, the more I think about it. You'd think they'd mention that on the pamphlet, but no.

"Just pretend we're in *Blue Velvet* or something," I'd try saying, turning out the lights as the luckiest girl in the whole wide world grabbed a pillow and headed for the couch.

I've had the CPAP machine a few years now, though I don't wear it every night. Sometimes it's just nice to wake up with nothing strapped to your face at all, like you're a completely normal person who doesn't snore like a bear and risk dying in his sleep or anything like that. And though it's pretty compact, I tend not to travel with it, either, not even when I'm visiting my dad, who I guess got me into this whole mess in the first place if you really think about it.

Not long ago, I was hanging out at his place when I fell asleep in front of the TV.

"You were snoring pretty loud while you were out," my dad told me when I eventually came to on his living room floor.

"I was?" I asked.

"Yes." He nodded. "That's sleep apnea for you."

"Yup," I said, nodding back.

"Like father, like son," he continued.

"Right," I agreed.

"I say that, of course, because we've both got it, you know," he continued. "Sleep apnea, that is."

"We sure do, Dad," I told him. "We sure do."

I kind of figured he might try to high-five me or something after that, but he just walked back into the kitchen to reheat his coffee in the microwave. And as he did so, it suddenly struck me, if he was going to pass something on to me, couldn't it have just been cash?

GIVING SOMETHING BACK

THERE ARE A LOT OF REASONS PEOPLE GO INTO SHOW business: money, sex, getting back at everybody from high school, having sex with everybody from high school, and probably a couple other reasons besides those, too. And while—trust me on this one—all that stuff is incredible, sometimes just a little recognition from others that, hey, you're doing a good job can also feel pretty good. And it is for this reason that, when I was asked to be on a panel of "industry professionals" at a weekend-long "entertainment workshop and seminar" just a couple subway stops from my apartment, I said, "Sure, I'll be there."

I suppose I should have seen the red flags from the beginning. For starters, the whole thing was being held at a small, hourly-rate dance studio across the street from the Port Authority bus station. It was also suggested that I think about bringing my own lunch, in case I got hungry and free candy just wasn't gonna cut it. But I tried not to let that stuff get to me. After all, I had worked hard to get where I was in my career as some apparently hard-to-categorize* combination of a comedian, writer, and musician who was living quite comfortably, thank you very much, in a rent-controlled fifth-floor walk-up studio apartment I was illegally subletting from a buddy of mine. The least I could do was give a couple hours of my time to help someone else maybe, just maybe, achieve at least some of the things I had managed to since moving out of my parents' house in suburban Cleveland a few years earlier.

The panel I was to appear on was advertised as the big finish of the entire two-day affair. Virtually every facet of show business, from not crying at auditions unless you've been asked to staging a one-man show even after everyone has begged you not to, would be covered in exacting detail, all leading up to that magic moment when I and a handful of other folks who, depending on whom you asked, had "made it" would show up to share a few of our trade secrets with the eager herd in attendance.

At least that's what I told myself.

Deep down inside, though, I knew I just wanted to be someplace for at least a little while where there would be some small guarantee that one or two people might make me feel that I was kind of special, that I wasn't just a failure, a fraud, an also-ran, or any of those other things I see in the mirror each day before I've had my coffee, facial, and meds.

I threw on a coat but no tie for the big day. I wanted to look put together but still approachable, kind of like those politicians who will take a teeny tiny sip of beer on camera at some point

---

* For others, I mean. As for me, I totally get it.

during their campaign to let everyone know that deep down inside they're just regular folks. When I walked into the dance studio, I could hear the sound of tap shoes attacking innocent floors and Broadway numbers being violated from various other studios on the floor. Somehow, even with my name on the flyer, the seminar I was asked to speak at had been taking place all weekend in a single one of these rooms. A little crazy, maybe, but it also gave things an air of exclusivity I kind of liked.

"We're running a little behind schedule," Tanya, the organizer of the whole thing, told me, ducking out into the hallway quickly before running back inside the room she had rented for the weekend. "Help yourself to some candy and I'll come grab you when this session wraps up."

I busied myself with a few Tootsie Rolls and a couple of those mini Reese's Peanut Butter Cups before Tanya opened the door again a few minutes later, releasing mostly air but also a couple attendees in the process.

"Not a problem," I thought. "I'm sure the four hundred or so people coming to *my* event will be stepping off the elevators at any minute."

"So," Tanya explained to me after waving good-bye to whomever, "attendance has been a bit lighter than expected for everything on the schedule this weekend."

"Not a problem," I thought. "I'm sure the two hundred or so people coming to *my* event will be stepping off the elevators at any minute."

When I finally stepped inside the studio Tanya had reserved for the event, though, I was met by, well, just Tanya, the other "industry professionals" on the panel, and one lone attendee, a short, bald man named Mark, who, while seemingly enthusiastic, failed in being the shitload of people I'd secretly been hoping for. I guess I shouldn't have been all that surprised, looking back on it. After all, my "fame," while a lot to shoulder both for me and the people I come in contact with most days, is also highly questionable when you really think about it.* I mean, sure, I am hands-down the most famous dude from my graduating high school class. But even so, you'd be surprised how easy it is for me to go grocery shopping, for example, without a single person, even the cashier, acknowledging me at any point. And as for my fellow panelists, they were without question very talented folks, every one of whom I greatly respected. But I don't think any of them would disagree when I say that they weren't the boldest of boldface names, either.

Keeping all of the above in mind, I figured it was at this point that Tanya might call us all into a huddle and delicately suggest that, rather than forge ahead with our audience of one, maybe we should just cut our losses, snatch up whatever was left of the free candy, and head over to Port Authority to go bowling or maybe catch the next bus to nowhere together. But instead she did the unthinkable.

"Well, the room is already paid for," she announced, "so why don't we make use of it somehow, unless, of course, anyone objects?"

It was at this point that I figured everyone in attendance, Mark included, would respond with a unanimous, perhaps even deafening "Yes! Let's get the hell out of here immediately and never speak of this day again!"

---

* And I have.

But somehow that didn't happen. And for whatever reason, I didn't speak up, either. So when Tanya asked that we all pull our chairs into a semicircle for some vague yet unquestionably sad discussion or another, I just held back the tears and grabbed the nearest folding chair.

"Maybe we could start by telling each other which venues we like and dislike in town," Tanya suggested, making my chest grow instantly tight. "Feel free to just jump right in."

"Well, I've been putting on some shows at this tiny space in an old church basement in Dumbo," a female performance artist with the tights to prove it said. "But it's been really hard to get people to come there for some reason."

"Maybe that's because it's a fucking tiny space in an old church basement in Dumbo," I wanted to say before instead just shaking my head like I didn't get non-artists these days for the life of me.

"I find having a solid mailing list really helps in situations like that," a burlesque comedian chimed in. "I'll send one e-mail a month before the show and then another maybe a week before the show."

"What about the day before the show?" Tanya asked. "Or even the day *of* the show?"

"Yeah." The burlesque comedian shrugged. "Sometimes I'll send another one then, too."

"And how do you make that decision?" Tanya followed up, furrowing her brow a bit to give the impression of genuine interest, like we were really getting somewhere.

"I guess I just sorta feel it out in my head," the burlesque comedian said. "Sometimes I'm just like 'Yeah, it feels like people are gonna come out to this one, probably' and other times I'm just like, 'Hmmm—maybe I better hit 'em up on e-mail again.'"

"That's really interesting," Tanya said, even though it definitely wasn't. "I love hearing about process."

It was at this point that Mark, the lone attendee mentioned earlier, began eating from a large bowl of soup that appeared seemingly from out of nowhere but had presumably been purchased from the Chinese place across the street beforehand. It took everything in my power to keep from reaching across the semicircle and strangling Mark as he did this, forcing the steaming-hot soup to spill from his mouth, down his chin, and all over the front of his heavily pilled sweater. I'm still not entirely sure why—part of it might have had to do with the fact that the free candy, just as I had been warned, really hadn't been enough. But I also think it was because the soup somehow made it seem like Mark was really in this for the long haul.

"Just keep talking," the look on his face seemed to suggest as he sat there, slurping attentively. "This soup will give me the sustenance I need to sit here in this semicircle long into the night until all of life's questions have been answered."

All of a sudden, I fucking hated Mark. And I hated everyone else in the room, especially Tanya, who had orchestrated this whole nightmare. But even more than Tanya, I hated myself for ultimately being so desperate for attention that I showed up here in the first place.

"This is my own damn fault," I thought as I sat there, staring a hole through Mark, his soup, and the packet of complimentary wontons that came with it, "and also, to some extent, the fault of my parents, who, if they would have just given me the love and attention I so deserved during my formative years, could have helped me avoid all this to begin with."

I honestly have no idea how much longer things went on after that. An hour? Six days? It's hard to say, really. The only thing I know for sure is that, by the time it was over, Mark had finished his soup and the performance artist had eaten at least half the party-sized bag of Cool Ranch Doritos that caused me a near seizure upon its unveiling. Regardless, at one point Tanya leaned forward to mercifully draw things to a close.

"We should probably wrap things up," she announced, setting her pen and clipboard into her lap with purpose.

"Thank God!" I thought. "Free at last!"

"So let's just take a quick bathroom break and meet back here in ten minutes for the show," she continued.

Oh, yeah. As part of this whole deal, after the panel session, where young hopefuls would in theory ask us "successful people" exactly how the hell we'd done it and exactly how the hell they might one day do it, too, we "pros" would put on a show for everybody in which we would all perform our slowly blackening hearts out.

"You deserve this, asshole!" I thought, kicking myself for ever having responded to the e-mail that got me here in the first place. "This will teach you to have fucking dreams or even a computer, for that matter!"

It was at this point that I got an idea. Maybe not a brilliant idea, but an idea just the same. First, I pulled out my phone and began pretending to scroll feverishly through my text messages.

"Oh, my God!" I then yelled. "Oh! My! God!"

"What is it?" the performance artist asked. "Dorito?"

"I'm sorry, I couldn't possibly tell you," I told her. "It's just . . . *too much*."

With this I slipped my phone back in my pocket and made a beeline for Tanya, who was busy asking Mark where he'd gotten the soup and if that place might still be open.

"I don't know how to tell you this, Tanya," I began in my best approximation of sheer panic, "but I j-just got a text from my friend D-David across town and and he . . . he s-somehow slipped and fell in his apartment and I'm the only other p-person who has keys to the place, so I have to go over there immediately to let the p-paramedics in before he loses c-consciousness."

"Oh, my God," Tanya said, appearing genuinely concerned, but probably mostly out of obligation. "Oh! My! God!"

It's hard to say whether she actually believed me. But I wanted to get out of there so badly I know I was starting to.

"Thanks for understanding," I told Tanya, placing my hands on her shoulder pads and squeezing gently for emphasis. "Have a great show! So sorry to miss it!"

A short elevator ride later, I found myself back out on Eighth Avenue among all the regular folks as they made their way along the sidewalk. Some shuffled lazily, others hurried anxiously, and a few just stood there, looking kind of drunk. But all were unremarkable, average, and totally anonymous.

And knowing that I was one them and nothing more was suddenly the greatest feeling in the world.

THE GREATEST

THERE'S AT LEAST A COUPLE SCENES IN EVERY CLINT Eastwood movie worth watching where some unlucky bastard manages to really push Clint's buttons, one thing leads to another, and Clint is left with no choice but to destroy the guy with his bare hands, shoot him in the face, or—at the very least—give him a stern talking-to he's not likely to forget anytime soon. And I don't care how much of a peace-loving wuss someone might be—whenever it happens in the movie, every single viewer can't help but think, "Yup—Clint handled that situation absolutely perfectly, and that sorry son of a bitch bleeding on the ground right now, struggling to maintain control of his bodily functions, got exactly what he deserved."

The very best examples of this sort of thing can, of course, be found in *Any Which Way You Can*, the 1980 sequel to the groundbreaking film *Every Which Way But Loose*, and easily the finest work of Clint Eastwood's entire career, if you ask me and a lot of other people, I bet. The film stars Eastwood in the role of Philo Beddoe, a well-meaning nut job with a penchant for mischief who fights in underground bare-knuckle boxing matches for money, which is awesome. In fact, that in itself would be the makings of a pretty great movie, but when you throw in the fact that Clint Eastwood's best friend in the movie just so happens to be a real live orangutan who goes by the name of Clyde,* you are suddenly dealing with one of the greatest films of all time, easily the *Citizen Kane* of movies that feature both Clint Eastwood and a fun-loving primate at the peak of their powers. Over the course of the film's nearly two hours, Clint and Clyde go everywhere together in Clint's rusty old pickup truck, at every turn kicking ass and getting up to all sorts of other hijinks, including covering an entire biker gang in tar, swinging from hotel room chandeliers,† and other stuff that is easily just as riveting as those two things. And no matter what sort of trouble Clyde gets up to on his own, it's not like Clint can ever stay mad at that hairy little scamp for long, which is just one more thing that makes this movie so, so great.

"Damn you, Clyde!" the look on Clint's face seems to say one moment. And then the next, Clint and Clyde are barreling down the road together in that truck again, smiling, laughing, and giving seemingly random people the finger, just two best buddies

---

* I don't know why, but the name Clyde really pushes things across the finish line for me in this case. They nailed it.

† Both Clint *and* the orangutan. It's great, and you won't want to miss it.

looking forward to whatever sort of orangutan-based excitement life has in store for them.

As for me, I've historically been a gentle type for the most part. Still, when I first saw *Any Which Way You Can* at a friend's birthday party back in elementary school, it was a veritable call to arms for the ten-year-old me.

"Oh, my God," I thought. "There's a whole world full of hard-core ass kicking out there that I've been missing out on this whole time."

When I returned home afterward, I couldn't wait to try and get my brother, Bob, to give me a reason to totally kick his ass all over the house, just like Clint did to pretty much every guy in that movie who wasn't an orangutan. The problem, of course, was that Bob was older, bigger, and stronger than I was and, at the first showing of aggression on my part, easily managed to send me screaming to the basement like a frightened schoolgirl, with a simple backhand. It was a hard lesson, but one I probably deserved, now that I sit here thinking about it. And between the fact that Bob had made it clear to me that he would swat me like a goddamn fly if I ever challenged him physically, mentally, or otherwise again, and that *Any Which Way You Can* ended up being the last film in that awesome franchise for some crazy reason I will never understand in a million years, it looked as if my violent urges had been quickly laid to rest.

Fortunately, however, all this was happening in the eighties, a decade in which professional boxing matches seemed to be on television just about every weekend. And it only took a couple Sunday afternoons in front of the tube to completely reawaken my unquenchable bloodlust. Sugar Ray Leonard, Larry Holmes, Marvin Hagler, some of the other ones. I watched them all intently, studying their every move, committing those moves to memory, and then just assuming that, should I choose to execute any of these moves on my own at a later date and time of my choosing, everything would go swimmingly. It took only a few weeks before I was fairly certain I might be the greatest practitioner of the "sweet science" currently enrolled in my grade school. I even had some of Muhammad Ali's classic taunts memorized and ready to break out at a moment's notice on anyone who would listen.

"Float like a butterfly, sting like a bee," I'd say while shadowboxing my grandmother, who was trying to read the paper. I forget what came after that, but I know it was enough to really upset the woman.

The only thing missing from this whole equation, of course, was a pair of boxing gloves, the key ingredient in my mission to punch another human being directly in the face and maybe, just maybe, get away with it. Fortunately, though, my dad made the mistake of swinging by the local department store for a lamp or some other household crap on the way home from a family outing one day, and as we wandered the aisles, I stumbled upon not one, but two pairs of boxing gloves, all sparkly and new and bundled together in a cardboard box I could only assume had been left there on the shelves for me by the gods. They were Everlast gloves and everything, the exact same brand I'd seen Sugar Ray Leonard and other guys with a taste for the rough stuff use to smack each other silly a thousand times before. The scent of their imitation leather was intoxicating. And the fact that my opponent's blood could be easily wiped off them with a damp rag was something I recognized and took comfort in immediately.

"All I need to do now is find myself a good cut man," I thought, pressing the box to my chest while still not entirely sure of what a cut man was. I couldn't wait to march the gloves to the checkout counter.

Unfortunately, though, my dad didn't seem nearly as pumped about the whole thing as I was.

"Put those down," he said, his voice lowering to suggest his tolerance for bullshit wasn't exactly great at the moment. "Now."

"But, Dad, you don't understand," I pleaded. "I really, really need these."

"No, you really, really don't," he replied. "Now let's go."

Since he was my ride home, I reluctantly set the gloves back down where I'd found them. But, being a young prick and all, I continued to beg my dad to buy me the gloves as we walked through the store. Still, he rejected my demands.

"Pleeeeaase g-get m-me the g-gloves, Daaaaaaad," I said, my begging slowly escalating to a full-on whining that even I could barely stand to be around. "I want them s-soooooo b-baaaaadly."

"No," my dad grunted, clearly annoyed and showing no signs that he was aware of being in the presence of a future boxing great, probably.

I'm not proud of what happened next, and this was the only time, I swear, that I have employed such a tactic since, while sober; but when neither my begging nor full-on whining managed to yield the desired result—the one where my dad totally buys me not one but two pairs of boxing gloves—I began to cry. And while, since then, I've certainly done many more pathetic things in my life, I'm happy to report that this particular performance was at least pathetic enough to get my dad to finally break down and pay for the damn gloves in an effort to shut me the hell up for at least the rest of the night.

"Fine," my dad said, begrudgingly retrieving his wallet from his coat pocket.

I felt kind of dirty and maybe even a little bit ashamed as we walked back to the car afterward, but I was certain it would all seem totally worth it when I was pummeling any and all takers with my new boxing gloves as they in turn tried and failed miserably to protect themselves with the other pair.

The next day, I raced out of the house to alert all of the other kids in the neighborhood of my good fortune. These were simpler times, and the youth of America had yet to be fully taken hostage by video games, the Internet, or anything else requiring electricity; so the sight of me showing up in my friend Kevin's driveway, where the boys of the neighborhood had already gathered to shoot hoops and talk smack about kids from the rival elementary school, with my brand-new boxing gloves was cause for considerable excitement.

"Check 'em out," I said, presenting the gloves to Brian, who, at sixteen, was the oldest of our group and therefore the kingpin.

"Pretty cool," he said, smacking his palm against the heavily padded gloves to simulate the sound of a human face being bashed in. "We should probably have some boxing matches."

"Yes," I agreed. "Yes, we should."

Everything was going exactly according to plan. I simply could not wait to beat the crap out of all my closest friends.

"You should probably fight first, since they're your gloves and all," Brian reasoned.

"Yeah, Dave, you fight first," the other kids said, nodding, presumably wanting to watch the master in action before they tried out the gloves for themselves.

Since Kevin's backyard was roughly the size of a regulation boxing ring, as best we could tell from what we'd seen on television, it was decided that that was where the fights should go down.

"Why don't you try fighting John?" Brian suggested as we all headed behind Kevin's house and descended on the thick crabgrass as if it were our very own Roman Colosseum.

John was my next-door neighbor, classmate, and best friend in the whole world, so it made perfect sense that I kick his ass first. Still, as I waited for the other kids to finish tying the gloves onto our puny fists, part of me couldn't help but feel bad about the merciless beating he was about to be handed. But that feeling was fleeting because, as soon as the other kids managed to jump out of the way, John began throttling my head, chest, stomach, and every other area of my body like some sort of prepubescent human jackhammer. If I hadn't known better, I would have sworn he had been waiting for this moment his whole life or at least since kindergarten.

"What kind of best friend punches you in the face that hard?" I wondered as I stood there, accepting the beating like I'd been born to do it. "And does he have to smile so wide as he does it?"

I was also struck by how completely different my new boxing gloves, these reluctant gifts from my dear father, my shelter from the storm, suddenly looked when they were coming directly at my face.

"Weren't they a whole lot softer back at the store?" I wondered as my brain seemed to bounce around inside my skull like a Ping-Pong ball. Now the gloves felt like rocks, and their odor all of a sudden seemed foul. And, worst of all, the sonorous *thud* they made every time they came in contact with my dewy, porcelain flesh seemed to be blatantly mocking me.

It's hard to say how long our boxing match lasted. Thirty seconds? Four hours? All I know is that once all the other kids in the yard seemed reasonably satisfied with the bludgeoning I'd just received, Brian jumped in to break things up.

"But I was j-just g-getting s-started," I whimpered as Brian shielded me from John's relentless attack.

"Oh, I know," Brian lied, peeling me off the ground. "I just wanted to give John a break."

"Yeah," I said, spitting grass and dirt from my teeth. "He s-seems tired."

"Can I try next?" Kevin blurted eagerly.

"Yeah, Kevin!" Pat, a sixth-grader from our neighborhood crew, agreed. "You beat up—I mean fight—Dave next!"

"Bring it on." I shrugged, determined to save face. "I'm just getting warmed up."

Kevin was in the fifth grade, too, and, like John, had a few pounds on me. Still, I was pretty sure everything I'd learned from watching boxing matches on television would snap into place and give me the upper hand this time. Also, Kevin had just moved into the neighborhood from what I considered a softer section of town, so I knew he lacked the street smarts and overall scrappiness instilled in John by a lifetime of playing golf on public courses and other indignities.

"This is gonna be easy," I thought as I bounced in place in my corner of our imaginary ring.

"Ding! Ding! Ding!" Brian yelled to start the bout.

I had been determined to make light work of Kevin, but he, like John, was surprisingly agile and weirdly aggressive, especially for a ten-year-old I had considered to be my second-best friend in the whole world, and managed to land what felt like sixty or seventy solid blows before I even had a chance to make it to the center of his backyard. And while I eventually succeeded in landing a couple punches myself, they seemed only to enrage Kevin further, which in turn led him to wallop me so hard that I flew straight through the pricker bushes bordering his yard and into Brian's yard next door, where I was surprised to find the beating still very much under way. There, temporarily out of sight from the rest of the neighborhood kids, Kevin then employed a couple wrestling-like moves that, I maintain to this day, were completely outside of regulations. The next thing I knew, I was flat on my back, trying and failing to stop Lance, the neighbor's amorous Siberian husky, from robbing me of my innocence right then and there.

"That's probably enough," Brian announced as he pulled Kevin and—eventually, with the help of some of the other kids—Lance off me.

With a couple losses under my belt, I assumed it was time to go home and perhaps re-strategize a bit. But unfortunately the drubbings I'd just received were like dumping chum into shark-infested waters and served only to further ignite the bloodlust of all the other kids hanging out in Kevin's backyard that day. Suddenly everyone was lining up for the chance to go toe-to-toe with little Dave Hill, this pale young thing with the increasingly high-pitched voice from Milford Road. Pat, Brian, Pat's older brother George, John's next-door neighbor Tommy, Kevin's older brother Danny, even a couple girls from the neighborhood whose curiosity had been piqued after hearing my screams echoing throughout the block—every single one of them eventually took a turn at strapping on my new boxing gloves and experiencing the special magic of making a human piñata out of me.

Finally, at around six o'clock, when Kevin's mom demanded that he and his brother Danny come inside for spaghetti night, the beatings came to an end.

"Darn," I said, struggling to my feet to begin the short limp home. "I was hoping we could keep fighting a while longer."

"We can pick it up tomorrow," Brian suggested. "It'll be fun."

"Totally," Kevin agreed.

"Yeah," I said, coughing. "It'll be so, *so* fun—thank you for suggesting it."

Cutting through Kevin's neighbor's yard, I was careful to steer clear of Lance, who, despite having gotten hold of an old tennis ball, had not convinced me that he had moved on emotionally from our earlier encounter. But there was no avoiding Mr. Mitchell, one of the neighborhood dads and a known smart-ass, as he trimmed the hedges in the next yard over.

"Well, if it isn't Muhammad Ali," he said, noting the boxing gloves hanging limply at my side as he momentarily switched off his electric clippers.

"You shut the hell up!" I mumbled as soon as he switched them back on.

I arrived home a couple minutes later to find my dad standing in the kitchen.

"Hey, Dave, you okay?" he asked, noting my face, which was as red and swollen as a baboon's ass after being clobbered by virtually every minor within five blocks of our house.

"Of course." I shrugged.

"Did everyone like your new boxing gloves?" he asked.

"Yes," I told him. "Maybe a little too much."

"I see," he said, creasing his brow.

The interrogation out of the way, I headed down to the basement to stuff my new boxing gloves deep into the closet we used to store old toys and other abandoned objects, where I was certain no one would discover them at least until the millennium.

"Why are you putting your brand-new boxing gloves all the way into the back of the closet like that?" my sister Katy, having appeared at the bottom of the basement stairs, asked suspiciously.

"Just letting 'em cool off a bit—all the greats do this," I replied, before slamming the closet door shut as hard as I could and heading for the stairs. "Ask anyone."

I've occasionally thought about those boxing gloves since that day. I've also thought about why my dad might have been so reluctant to buy them for me in the first place. Was he just trying to avoid spending the money? Or did he somehow know exactly what would happen once we brought them home, that they would instantly be used against me just as soon as the rest of the kids in the neighborhood laid eyes on them? Recently, I decided to find out.

"Remember those boxing gloves you bought me back when I was a kid?" I asked.

"Yeah," he said, and chuckled.

"What's so funny?" I asked.

"Well, I definitely wouldn't have bought them for you if I had to do it all over again," he replied.

I'm not sure what the hell that was supposed to mean. Still, looking back on it, I can't say I disagree with him. After all, what I really wanted was to live in a world where, if I ever did get into a fight, I always had the option of having my best friend who also happened to be an orangutan step in and finish the job for me.

MESSAGE IN A BOTTLE

A S MENTIONED PREVIOUSLY IN THIS IMPORTANT BOOK, I moved back to New York City in 2003 after an extended hiatus spent holding things down in majestic Cleveland. And in the time that I've been back in New York, high on the list of complaints I hear people make about this town is that it's lost its edge. As I think back to the days when I could wander the streets of Manhattan openly pounding a forty-ounce beer in broad daylight before tossing the empty bottle to the ground, unzipping my pants, and relieving myself on the sidewalk just to break up the monotony a little, I can't say I disagree. Nowadays you can't really get away with any of that stuff without someone calling the cops or at least 311. But you *can* get a really nice brunch just about anywhere in the five boroughs. It's a give-and-take when you get right down to it.

The reason I bring all this up is a little while back I was asked to take part in a show out in Brooklyn, a tribute to the German electronic band Kraftwerk, who were playing a sold-out show at the Museum of Modern Art across the river in Manhattan that same night. It was to be a classy affair, complete with a performance by Kim Gordon from Sonic Youth, all-you-can-eat pizza backstage, and other stuff, too. In hopes of rising to the occasion, I threw on a suit and tie and spent as much time on my hair as my schedule would possibly allow.

I was about to head down into the subway station at Twenty-Eighth and Broadway to take the R train to Brooklyn when from out of nowhere I was overcome by a powerful hunger.

"Oh, man," I thought, "I honestly don't know if I can hold out for that contractually agreed-upon pizza anymore—I think I need to grab something right now before I keel over, Metrocard in hand."

Luckily, there was a gyro stand directly outside the subway station. I decided to make a beeline for it.

"Gimme one gyro with everything," I told the gyro guy in a manner I hoped would suggest I meant business. "And don't hold back on the sauces, either."

With this, the gyro guy sprang to action, whipping up a gyro the size of a small terrier in a matter of seconds. I ripped it from his latex-covered mitts, handed him some cash, and ran down into the subway station, where a train was just rolling up to the platform. I jumped into the nearest car, tore open the gyro wrapper, and began attacking the Greek delicacy as soon as the doors closed. Unfortunately, though, the gyro guy had taken my request about not holding back on the sauces a little too seriously, and as a result, a medley of yogurt, garlic, and chili sauces began oozing from the gyro as soon as I took a bite, causing them to run all over my hands and down onto the floor of the subway car. It suddenly occurred to me that the funk of the gyro meat was probably filling the entire jam-packed, rush-hour train now, too.

"That guy looks incredible," I imagined my fellow passengers thinking as they glared at me and the mess I was making. "But it's not very cool of him to eat a gyro on the train during rush hour like that."

Bearing that in mind, I decided the best thing I could do under the circumstances was to get off the train at the next station and finish my gyro before continuing to Brooklyn. So as the train pulled into Twenty-Third Street, I hopped off and walked all the way to end of the platform to finish my gyro in relative solitude next to one of those black metal storage bins* they seem to have at the end of most New York subway platforms.

I devoured the rest of the gyro as quickly as possible, but was left with the yogurt, garlic, and chili sauce–covered wrapper to dispose of. I scanned the platform for a trash can but there was none. It was too messy to stuff in my pocket, so, not wanting to toss it on the ground or on the train tracks, I figured the best thing I could do under the circumstances was to set it down on top of the black metal storage bin.

"That way whoever has to clean it up later won't have to bend over to pick it up," I thought, setting the wrapper down thought-

---

* In the interest of clarity, let me point out that I am referring to a totally regular black metal storage bin, and not a Norwegian black metal storage bin, in this instance. However, I would be the first to admit that having a Norwegian black metal storage bin at the end of each subway platform in New York would basically be the coolest thing ever and I would have no problem whatsoever with having my tax dollars spent to make that dream an awesome reality.

fully. "They can just knock it into their trash bag and keep on a-movin'. Who knows? It might even be kind of fun for them."

As you can probably imagine, I was pretty proud of my problem-solving skills at that point, but before I even had a chance to bask in the moment, I all of a sudden heard a rustling from the other side of the storage bin. As it turned out, a homeless man had been sleeping on the other side, and my thoughtful gyro wrapper disposal had somehow woken him.

"Back up!" he screamed in my direction as he struggled to his feet, his long hair protruding from his head every which way, like stalagmites.

I figured the next train would be pulling into the station any second, so I didn't see much sense in honoring his request.

"I'll be gone momentarily and we can both just get back to living our lives," I thought.

But the homeless guy, seemingly growing angrier by the millisecond, wasn't having it.

"Back up!" he screamed again.

"What's this guy possibly gonna do if I don't move?" I thought, still holding my ground.

"Back up!" he screamed a third time.

It seems worth noting at this point that the man in question here seemed pretty darn homeless, at least as far as guys who take naps on subway platforms go, anyway—I didn't get the sense that this was just some sort of phase he was going through. And, as a result, it occurred to me, given what I perceive to be a prevalence of active imaginations in the homeless community, that he may very well be screaming at an imaginary person who just so happened to be standing right where I was at the time.

"Back up," the homeless guy screamed a fourth time, "or I'll throw this bottle of piss on you!"

Suddenly he had my attention. And in his left hand he indeed held a large Gatorade bottle. It was no ordinary Gatorade bottle, either—it was the largest Gatorade bottle I had ever seen, the kind I assume to be favored by people who refuse to drink any liquid other than Gatorade under any circumstances ever, only instead of being filled with the popular sports drink, it was full of urine.*

"Sure thing," I thought to say to the homeless guy. "It would be my pleasure to back up straight on out of this subway station right now if you so desire, my good man."

But before I had the chance, he'd already cocked his arm back and launched the entire contents of the massive Gatorade bottle straight at me. There it was, this arc of buttery hobo pee coming at me like a fire hose. And, homeless or not, not a drop was wasted. His aim, in fact, was impeccable.

I managed to turn quickly enough so as not to get blasted directly in the face, but not quickly enough to spare my luscious locks from the assault.

"All that hard work for nothing," I thought, my hair instantly falling limp.

Other casualties, aside from my dignity, included my jacket,

---

* For those of you not personally familiar with the mechanics of urinating into a bottle, whether it be of the Gatorade variety or perhaps some other electrolyte-restoring beverage, it's worth noting that it would likely take—by my well-informed estimation, anyway—roughly two or three weeks to fill a bottle this size. If you factor in that the homeless are a historically dehydrated people, that number jumps easily to four or five weeks. Please bear this in mind as you continue reading.

trousers, and underwear. That is correct—this man had effectively wet *my* pants with *his pee*.

"Well played," I thought, just giving credit where credit was due.

By now, of course, everyone else on the subway platform had begun scurrying in all directions in hopes of getting as far away as possible from the homeless guy and me, his piss-drenched nemesis, who was now flailing around like Jennifer Beals in that one scene in *Flashdance* when someone dumps an entire bucket of water on her for ultimately sexy reasons.

It's at this point that I thought to perhaps retaliate in some way, but then it hit me: if my opponent's first move in a confrontation is to soak me in his own urine, what other tricks might he have up his sleeve?

"At the very least he's gotta have a couple more bottles of pee locked and loaded back behind that storage bin," I thought before deciding maybe the wisest thing to do at this point was to just bid the man adieu and take my leave.

"Touché," I thought as I shuffled toward the exit.

Moments later, I found myself standing on the corner of Fifth Avenue and Twenty-Third Street as whatever was left of the homeless guy's pee continued running down my body in tiny rivulets. I figured getting a cab might not be the most viable or considerate option, both in light of the traffic and my current condition, so I decided to just walk down Fifth Avenue in the direction of home, a shower, and a suit with less pee on it. Meanwhile, the pee that had managed to nail me in the head had begun to gather at the ends of my hair in little droplets, framing my face kind of like a headdress one of those old-timey flappers might have worn. It was still early, and the sun was still out. And as I continued walking home, the light of the sun began passing through those little droplets of pee. And as they did, tiny little prisms and beautiful rainbows began to form inside those droplets. As I squinted up at them, I became instantly transfixed. And it was in that moment that all the pain and anger just fell away. Because it was in that moment that I realized something . . .

This motherfucking town is back.

ALL THINGS MUST PASS

I WAS SITTING AT HOME THINKING ABOUT GETTING killer abs one day when my dad called to tell me that he had just returned from the dietician's office at his retirement community with some unsettling news. As it turned out, he was suddenly among the roughly six billion people worldwide currently being held hostage by a gluten allergy, the single greatest killer of our time.

"Are you sure?" I asked him, trying to break the silence.

"Well, the dietician sure seems to think so," my dad answered resignedly.

This wasn't the first run-in my dad had had with food or anything. He'd been making a conscious effort to steer clear of wheat since at least the nineties. And while he wasn't lactose intolerant, he wasn't exactly crazy about it, either. Still, between the fact that he had recently lost his wife, packed up and moved his entire life for the first time in over forty years, and was most likely about to be hit up for money again by me, I figured a new health concern was the last thing my dad needed at this point, so I did my best to stay positive. First, I tried to tell him that—technically speaking, anyway—only 1 percent of the population actually suffers from celiac disease, the cruel, unforgiving, and sometimes even gas-inducing monster behind this far less intimidating-sounding "gluten allergy" my dad's dietician had obviously tried to cushion the blow with, and that maybe, just maybe, she was completely wrong in her diagnosis. I also reminded him of all the great times we'd had together enjoying stuff like bagels, crackers, and even bread sticks over the years. I even pointed out that he was eighty-two years old and had been living a carefree, gluten-filled life all this time, so screw it, why stop now? But he wouldn't hear a word of it.

"Gluten and I are through," he said. "That's just how it's gotta be from now on."

"Well, do your best to hang in there," I said supportively before hanging up the phone. "I know you can beat this thing."

My dad has never been one for trends, so I hoped he might quickly grow tired of the gluten-allergy craze he had suddenly become swept up in. But when I hopped a plane to Cleveland a few weeks later, I found things even worse than expected. Not only had all forms of bread, cereal, pasta, and even flour tortillas been eradicated from his home and—I'm assuming—torched out back in some sort of ritualistic, gluten-shaming bonfire, but their absence was magnified by the fact that they had all been replaced with their 100 percent gluten-free and also totally sucky counterparts. There was gluten-free bread, gluten-free cereal, gluten-free pasta, you name it. He even managed to find products that had been labeled gluten-free, even though the original versions didn't have any gluten in them in the first place, and everyone knows it. It was nuts.

"If you're hungry, you can help yourself to some toast or whatever," my dad said as I quietly assessed the damage.

"Yeah, right—like I'm gonna eat a fucking piece of gluten-free toast," I thought to tell him. But since I didn't want to risk getting grounded, I suggested we go out to eat instead, preferably somewhere with at least a few 100 percent gluten options on the menu that I might order in an effort to balance out the universe.

"We can try," my dad said. "But it can be tricky with this gluten allergy."

Tricky was an understatement. Whereas my dad and I used to just hop in his Buick and go get ourselves pizza, spaghetti, muffins, and just about anything else whenever we damn well pleased, to even suggest most of these things now was tantamount to my grabbing a knife from the kitchen and plunging it through his chest repeatedly until the cops arrived—at least to hear him tell it anyway.

"I can't even look at most of the stuff they have at Panera anymore," he added, staring out the window as if he were in some old French film.

"Panera blows anyway," I told him, admittedly just looking to talk shit about Panera. "What about Mexican?"

"Flour tortillas," he replied matter-of-factly. "Can't do it."

"You can get corn tortillas instead," I offered.

"Corn might have gluten in it," he said. "I'm not sure."

The answer, he explained, was unfortunately on some sheet of paper the dietician had given him that was now buried under a bunch of other stuff and could take hours, maybe even days, to find. And while I probably could have Googled the answer on my phone, that also felt like too much work, so instead we just settled on a Middle Eastern restaurant near his apartment, since, pita bread aside, chances were slim I'd have to drag a corpse out of the place at the end of our meal.

We'd been to the Middle Eastern joint before. The menu was decidedly health conscious with several pages dedicated to vegetarian and even fully vegan options. There was even a separate smoothie menu where, for only a dollar or two more, you could add shots of various ingredients that enable you to feel superior to others. In short, it was kind of a lame restaurant when you got right down to it. Making matters worse, my dad couldn't help but ask our waitress if there was any chance gluten was present in every single one of the items he was even thinking about ordering, even though virtually every item on the menu had a little GF next to it to signify the absence of this potentially murderous thickening agent he and so many others were on the run from.

"I think you'll find most of the items on our menu are gluten-free," she said proudly, as if it were an idea she had come up with all by herself on the way back from Burning Man or something.

"The reason I ask is because I have a gluten allergy," he told her, as if the mere mention of it might qualify him for a complimentary slice of gluten-free cake they'd been keeping in the back for just such an occasion, as a sort of Make-A-Wish Foundation arrangement they'd set up for people likely to experience bloating, abdominal discomfort, or even full-on pants-shitting during their meal.

"Me, too!" our waitress replied before excitedly skipping back to the kitchen to hand over our order to the cook and probably sneak a quick shot of wheatgrass or some other crap while she was at it.

In the end, my dad ordered a mostly non-threatening vegetarian chili and I ordered some sort of grilled meat on a stick with a side of hummus in case I felt like getting nuts.

"Have you ever been tested for a gluten allergy?" my dad asked, seemingly looking to bond as our entrées arrived a few minutes later.

"No, but I've definitely lost a few friends to gluten in the last couple years," I said.

"What do you mean?" he asked.

"Never mind," I replied before trying to trick him into eating some pita bread.

We finished our meals without incident before passing on dessert and staring at each other for a full ten minutes after the check arrived until one of us reluctantly agreed to pay it.

Back at my dad's apartment a while later, I ended up sneezing a couple times while we tried to decide what to not really watch on TV.

"You have a cold?" my dad asked.

"No," I said. "I think it's the pollen or something."

"Are you sure it's not a wheat allergy?" he asked. "I've had a wheat allergy for years."

"Isn't that the same thing as a gluten allergy?" I asked him.

"No, a wheat allergy is completely different," he said. "It really wouldn't surprise me if you had one."

"I don't think so," I said.

"You might think about getting tested, just to be safe," he

replied. "A lot of people walk around with a wheat allergy for years and they don't even know it."

"That's terrifying," I said.

"I know," my dad said. "And then of course there is a dairy allergy, which is a whole other thing."

I pretended not to hear that last part and quickly changed the topic to a rumor I'd heard about some guy in my dad's building who had an adverse reaction to cocktail peanuts. Later that night, after I was sure my dad was asleep, I borrowed his car and snuck into town for a personal pan pizza and a sleeve of saltines and my dad couldn't say shit about it.

SOME PEOPLE WERE
KUNG FU FIGHTING

BACK WHEN I WAS A KID GROWING UP ON THE MEAN streets of suburban Cleveland, my dad used to take my siblings and me to the public library every Saturday. He'd park the car out front, and before he'd even have a chance to warn us about not getting caught flipping through old issues of *National Geographic* again, we'd all run inside and get lost in the stacks.

While my sisters usually gravitated toward the latest Nancy Drew caper or maybe something by one of those Brontë nut jobs, and my brother buried his nose in books about history, firearms, or home taxidermy, I always headed straight for the sports section, where at the very bottom of the shelf sat a small collection of books about the martial arts. Tomes on karate, kung fu, tae kwon do, judo, jujitsu, even that Krav Maga bullshit—they were all there, waiting to be devoured by me, the steeliest young grasshopper in all of the east side suburbs of Cleveland, as far as I was concerned. I feverishly flipped through the pages, convinced that one day I'd end up in books just like these—preferably shirtless and with the blood of my enemies streaming down my 100 percent fat-free torso and pooling at my feet as some smoking-hot chick stood in the background, just trying to contain herself at the very sight of me. I'd change my mind over and over again about exactly which discipline I'd master in record time as a means to eventually killing with my bare hands and hopefully also feet without even really trying.

"Can I pleeeease take (insert name of whichever martial art I thought was the "best" that week here) lessons?" I'd beg my dad on the drive home.

I imagine he thought it was pretty cute, just the fleeting fancy of a boy left unattended in front of a Saturday-afternoon kung fu movie one too many times. But the truth is I was hell-bent on becoming a martial arts wizard, splitting cinder blocks in two with my pinky, knocking opponents to the ground just by blinking at them, growing a crazy-ass mustache, and—who knows—maybe even moving out of my parents' house one day. And I was determined not to let the dream die despite the fact that my dad would always turn up the radio really loud whenever I brought it up. As these things often go, eventually I caught a few rounds of the Masters on television, demanded that my dad immediately drop me off at the nearest putt-putt course, and never brought up the whole killing-with-my-bare-hands thing again.

Recently, however, it occurred to me that I was officially staring down, or at the very least standing right next to, the barrel of middle age. Sure, I tried to deny it. But with every friend who suddenly let me know he was getting divorced or remarried, every time I got invited out to some job-having bastard's "summer home" for the weekend, and every doctor who approached me with a gloved hand and gelled finger without warning because I was "getting to that age and it was important to keep tabs on that sort of thing regardless of my deductible," I began to accept that I'd officially be on the back nine of this crazy thing called life faster than you can request a high chair at Ruby Tuesday. And with that, I decided it was time to stop thinking about myself for a change and start thinking about that little Dave Hill still inside me somewhere, that innocent imp who figured he'd be sitting cross-legged on a mountain in the Himalayas with a long white ponytail and flowing gown by now, meditating peacefully until it was time to go knock some jackass's eyeball out of his head in one swift blow. In short, it was time to cut the crap and start following my fucking dreams.

I did a little sniffing around, and word on the street (and also Google) had it that for years now one of the greatest kung fu masters on the entire planet had been turning guys like me into walking death machines at a place called the USA Shaolin Temple, conveniently located less than two miles from my apartment. As the story goes, the guy who founded the place, Shi Yan Ming, came to America from China as part of a first-ever Shaolin Temple monks tour of the United States back in the early nineties. After the last show of the tour in San Francisco, Shi Yan Ming snuck out of his hotel room in the middle of the night to start a new life for himself in America, eventually making his way to New York City, the perfect place for that sort of thing.

The fact that the most badass thing I ever snuck out of my hotel room in the middle of the night for was to see if they'd accidentally left out the Froot Loops dispenser from the complimentary Continental breakfast the morning before made me feel kind of lame by comparison. And when I learned that Shi Yan Ming had even taught kung fu to one of the guys from the Wu-Tang Clan,* I decided to just go ahead and take a wild detour on my way home from Bed Bath & Beyond over to that temple of his.

"Your life starts today, my friend," I said to myself as I caught my reflection in a store window and imagined how incredible I'd probably look with one of those cool hairstyles where your whole head is shaved except for a long braided ponytail in the back.

I swear I could already feel my transformation into a kung fu master beginning on the walk over to the temple. My posture was improved and my stride a bit more purposeful. And when people bumped into me on the street, instead of just giving them the finger once I was sure they weren't looking, I practiced targeting their vital organs with my mind.

The temple was located on the second floor of an old industrial building on Broadway, right above a shoe store that sold discount footwear in all the latest styles. As soon as I walked in, I could tell this Shi Yan Ming guy wasn't messing around. There was a giant, seemingly irritated dragon painted on the far wall and cool Asian stuff as far as the eye could see. There was even a barrel of swords, axes, and other shiny weaponry that guys like me could

---

* You know, the popular Staten Island rap group featuring RZA, GZA, Method Man, Raekwon, Ghostface Killah, Inspectah Deck, Ol' Dirty Bastard (RIP), U-God, Masta Killa, and Capadonna, that I would be totally down to hang out with sometime soon if any of them happens to be reading this right now. Just putting it out there. Also, thanks for reading my book, guys. How cool is that?

presumably employ to take things to the next level sitting in the corner, begging to be called into action. For maybe the first time in my life, I felt like I was home.

With class about to start, the students were slowly filing in.

"*Amituofo*," a squat Hispanic guy of about thirty said to me, bowing slightly and folding his hands at his chest like a praying mantis as we made eye contact.

At first I thought he might have been starting some shit with me, but it turned out that *amituofo* is simply a Mandarin greeting everyone at the temple uses so often you'd swear they were getting paid by the syllable. I couldn't blame them, either—as I soon learned, *amituofo*, besides being fun to say, is even more versatile than the F-word. It can mean "peace," "hello," "goodbye," and even "get the hell out of my way before I stab you or at least hurt your feelings," if you say it just right. In short, it's really great and I couldn't wait to start using it myself as soon as possible.

For a small donation, the temple lets visitors sit in on a class and decide for themselves if they're ready to be transformed into a one-man apocalypse, as if I were even questioning that shit for a second. I'd expected all the regular students to look just like the guys I'd seen in kung fu movies, their bodies taut, their heads shaved, and their facial expressions frozen in a look that at once suggested inner peace and also that they wouldn't think twice about ripping your heart out from your chest and holding it in the air right in front of you, still beating as the life drained from your eyes, in one lightning-fast, blood-drenched motion. But instead, most of them looked like just about the last people you'd expect to be training as barefoot assassins. There was a pudgy

African American woman with John Lennon glasses in one corner, a transgendered person with a dangling feather earring in another, and even a potbellied Gene Shalit look-alike I'm still not entirely convinced was not actually Gene Shalit slowly doing random and odd, martial arts–looking stretches as they waited for class to get under way. I was a little confused at first, but then realized that this was just one more thing that makes kung fu so awesome—that element of surprise.

"There's no way in hell Gene Shalit is going to kill me with his bare hands," his foolish and unworthy opponent thinks.

But the next thing the foolish and unworthy opponent knows, he's flat on his back in a pool of his own blood, his whole life flashing before him, as Gene Shalit calmly saunters off into the horizon without having compromised his mustache in the slightest.

"Man, this is going to be great," I thought, suddenly taking pride in how non–kung fu–like I must have looked to the untrained eye as I stood there fishing my sweat pants out of my butt.

Just as I was beginning to come up with a few cool stretches of my own without even really trying, Shi Yan Ming, or *shifu*, meaning "master," as he is known to his disciples, suddenly appeared, seemingly from out of nowhere, in the corner of the room, looking exactly as I'd hoped he would, in one of those bright orange Shaolin monk robes I'd seen in the movies. He stood calmly, scanning the room as if he couldn't decide whether or not he felt like teaching class that day or slaughtering all fifteen or so of us in attendance before meeting up with one of his Shaolin monk buddies for a sandwich or whatever those sick fucks get up to when they hang out together. When he suddenly screamed something in Mandarin I couldn't understand, I assumed *shifu* had decided on the latter, and I began looking for cover. But when everyone began assembling in a row across the padded floor, I was relieved to find out I'd be getting my forty bucks' worth of murder training, after all.

"Just do your best to imitate the moves everyone else is doing," an assistant at the temple told me before class.

"If by 'imitate' she means being about fifty times more awesome than, that shouldn't be a problem," I thought before bowing and mispronouncing *amituofo* a couple times in her direction.

Up until this point in my life, I'd assumed the graceful yet ideally deadly motions involved with kung fu would come naturally to me, not unlike the way a newborn foal just goes tearing across a meadow at blinding speed alongside its mother only moments after some stable boy finishes hosing off the placenta and other baby horse gunk. In reality, though, my actions were surprisingly stiff, perhaps even a bit awkward, depending on whom you ask. In fact, only one area of my body was moving very freely at all. And with that I made a mental note to pick up a jockstrap before the next class.

"More chi!"* *shifu* suddenly yelled, scaring the crap out of me as I attempted to kick toward the ceiling so hard I feared I might need ass surgery later.

"Train harder!" all the students except me yelled back at him.

As it turned out, this was the official call-and-response man-

---

* *Chi* or *qi* is a Chinese word meaning "life energy." It's kind of like "The Force" from *Star Wars* but way cooler and with better outfits.

tra of the temple, the Shaolin equivalent of "no pain, no gain." And as the class progressed, the students themselves began taking the lead with the chant.

"More chi!" the Gene Shalit look-alike would scream without warning.

"Train harder!" everyone would respond, trying to outdo each other in volume, enthusiasm, and overall kung fu–ness. It happened over and over again to the point where I wanted to add my own third part to the mantra, something along the lines of "Okay, let's just take it down a notch, everybody!" before remembering I was the new guy and realizing this may be interpreted as a physical challenge. As best I could tell, everyone in the class was American, but I also noticed that the more they all screamed, the more they seemed to take on a Chinese accent themselves while doing so. It struck me as perhaps a bit racist at first, but before long I found myself screaming right along with them, as if I had just rolled into town from Shanghai that morning. I have to admit, it felt pretty great, too.

The class that day lasted two hours but it felt like six to eight weeks. And while I was completely wiped out by the end of it, it was a good kind of wiped out, the kind those Shaolin monk guys in their cool-ass orange robes and sweet haircuts felt all the time, I was guessing.

In my exhaustive research, I'd read that Hong Kong movie stars and kung fu masters Jackie Chan and Sammo Hung were required to train so hard in their youth that they'd be severely punished if they had to use the bathroom afterward. Apparently the idea was that you were supposed to sweat everything out during your workout—your bladder should never even come into the equation, unless you were some kind of wuss. And while I didn't quite get to that level right away, when I hit the men's room after class, I felt encouraged when I discovered I had somehow ripped my boxers almost completely in half during class.

"I bet this sort of thing happened to Jackie and Sammo a lot, too," I thought as I collapsed on the couch back home afterward, my secret parts spilling freely out of my underpants and onto the stain-resistant velveteen. "Who knows? Maybe I'll stop wearing underpants altogether once this kung fu business really kicks in with me." The future seemed bright. Really, *really* bright.

That night, I called my dad to tell him the good news, that I had finally decided to harness the power of my dreams and become the kung fu master I knew I was destined to be. Inexplicably, he just laughed. Maybe it was a test. Or maybe he was just being a jerk. Either way, I told him I'd call him later in the week when it was a better time to talk maybe. Then I hung up the phone and made a mental note to mail him the vital organs of the first person who crossed me after I got done with kung fu lessons.

I resumed my training at the temple the following Tuesday, intentionally cutting through graffiti-covered alleys and walking past especially dangerous-looking Chipotles along the way in hopes of running into an entire street gang in need of a good ass-kicking or at least a stern talking-to. And when I arrived at the temple, I bowed and said *amituofo* to everyone in sight, like I'd invented it.

There were a lot of the same students from the other day at the temple already, as well as a few new faces, including a mother with a son in tow who appeared to be about six years old. Based on what I'd learned from all the kung fu movies I'd ever seen, I knew it's usually best to start the beat-downs with the youngest in the family and work your way up from there. But it turned out the kid wasn't actually taking the class, so I decided to let him live. For now.

"You have no idea how lucky you are, kid," I thought, glaring at him quickly while his mother wasn't looking. To be honest, I don't think he saw me, either, as he seemed pretty caught up in a handheld video game at the time. God, I hated that kid.

In an effort to fit in a bit more at the next class, I ended up buying the temple's official workout gear: matching, loose-fitting navy pants and top, a maroon T-shirt with some cool Chinese writing on it, and some special kung fu shoes, presumably designed to make kicking holes through people's chests a bit easier, that were a sparkling white I assumed was only temporary.

"Soon these will be caked in the blood of my adversaries," I thought as I fastened the shoes with big bunny-ear knots.

As I hit the workout mat in my new outfit, I was practically levitating with excitement.

"More chi!" *shifu* yelled again, getting class under way.

"Tray hodda!" the entire class, myself included, shouted in response, by now sounding as if we were no longer aware the English language had ever even existed.

This being my second class and all, I figured I'd learn to properly crack rib cages or crush a skull or two, but the session consisted of more of the same contact-free kicking, jumping, spinning, and determined whipping of arms I'd attempted during the first class. I did learn that each individual move had a really cool name, but I could never seem to remember or even pronounce it, no matter how many times everyone repeated it really loudly and slowly to me, like I'd just been cured of deafness by a televangelist. Between that and the fact that I had yet to even graze another human being, I was starting to get a little frustrated. But then I remembered how patient David Carradine always seemed in those old episodes of *Kung Fu* in the role of Shaolin badass Kwai Chang Caine, even when that old blind guy would go on and on about some crazy shit that didn't make any sense at all.

"Focus, not quite middle-aged grasshopper," I told myself as I steadied myself on the mat with renewed determination. "One day this shall all come back to you tenfold."

As *shifu* observed us, he would occasionally break out some moves of his own without warning, as though he had an especially awesome form of Tourette's syndrome or something. His kicks were so high, hard, and fast, it was like he was from another dimension.

"I wonder if *shifu* ever rips his underwear," I thought as I stood there, marveling. It occurred to me to just come out and ask him, but I felt we weren't quite there yet. Besides, before I had the chance, he was waving at me to step out of line.

"Mister," he said to me in a manner that somehow sounded at once respectful and condescending, "come over here."

I figured this was it, the moment he just goes and kicks my ass in front of everybody to teach me a lesson I wouldn't even begin to understand until I got out of the ER or he would at least make me go wash his car with weirdly specific instructions or something, but then he called over one of the other, more experienced students and asked him to demonstrate to me the move we had just been working on—I can't remember what the hell it was called—one-on-one. It was only my second class and I had apparently already been identified as a "special needs" student.

As the student, a tall, sinewy fellow with a ponytail that suggested an enthusiasm for jam bands, carefully walked me through each part of the maneuver, I thought to give him a quick chop to the Adam's apple just to let him know who he was dealing with, but I knew there was no way I was ever going to get my deposit back that way. So instead I just listened closely for a few minutes before spending the rest of the class practicing the move on my own over and over again while all the other students continued flying through the air and screaming in broken English on the other side of the room.

"I bet even Bruce Lee struggled at first," I thought, trying to comfort myself before scratching my chest as hard as I could in an attempt to draw blood when I was pretty sure no one was looking.

It turned out I had ripped my boxers in two during that class, too. Between that and the fact that I was determined to find some practical application for the few moves from class I could remember, I prayed that somebody, anybody, would somehow cross me on the walk home that day. A hot dog vendor, a junior high student, even an old lady carrying groceries—it didn't matter. I just wanted a fight.

"Surely someone in this town needs to be taught a goddamn lesson," I thought as I shot a dirty look at anyone willing to make eye contact. But unfortunately there were no takers. And as I collapsed on my bed a half hour later, my kung fu outfit in a sad, sweaty ball on the floor, I knew the only one who had been defeated that day was me.

That night, in an effort to get super-psyched for the next class, I watched a few kung fu videos on YouTube, including one where a Shaolin monk dragged a barrel across the ground with his scrotum and another where a Shaolin monk let some other guy kick him over and over again right in the clangers like it was no big deal.* It was awesome.

"Stick with it, Dave," I told myself as I watched the monk stare blankly into the distance like he had horrible seats at an Eagles concert while some other guy lodged his foot into the monk's crotch so many times it was as if the video were on a loop. "This is *really* going to pay off someday."

Sore all over and feeling a little loopy from an old muscle relaxer I'd found on the bathroom floor, I trudged back to a third class a couple days later, this time not even bothering to look for any fights or to bring anyone to justice on the way over.

"I just don't need the hassle right now," I told myself. But the truth is, there was a very small part of me that was starting to doubt whether I really had what it takes to become a kung fu master, after all. Sure, I had the body—anyone would agree with that. And my mental focus made Uri Geller† look like an Adderall candidate. But between the fact that the temple was almost a half hour's walk from my apartment and the long naps I'd require after each class, a certain weariness had begun to set in.

---

* I strongly encourage you to momentarily put down this book and go look up both of these videos and watch them closely right now. They really put things in perspective no matter what's going on in your life. Go ahead, do it. I'll be right here. Waiting.

† Famed spoon bender and friend of Michael Jackson.

"This is only level one—at this rate it could be years before I get to even *try* to kick someone in the head," I thought. "Maybe there was a reason David Carradine skipped out on that Shaolin monastery in *Kung Fu*. You know, besides the fact that everyone wanted to kill him."

I tried not to show any signs of uncertainty when I walked into the temple a few minutes later, but when I responded to a fellow student's usual *amituofo* by saying "'Sup" followed by a half-assed wave, I figured at least a couple people must have been onto me.

As class got under way, it occurred to me to maybe just attack *shifu* the second he walked out onto the mat.

"He'll either kill me instantly or respect my enthusiasm and decide to take me under his wing," I reasoned.

But then I imagined the phone call notifying my family of what happened, and quickly lost my nerve.

"That's right, Dave's heart was ripped directly from his chest," a representative from the temple would explain to whoever picked up the phone. "But we are happy to report that we will be issuing you a full refund on all the classes he has already paid for, not including the one he got killed in, of course. You take care now!"

Instead, I just fell in line with the rest of the students as soon as things got started.

The third class consisted of all the same moves and exercises we worked on before, with the surprising addition of cartwheels, something I could never do as a child and—as I quickly learned— still couldn't do all these years later. As a kid, I'd rationalized my inability by just telling myself they were "for girls." But, standing in the temple as an adult and, if anything, actually being even worse at them now was downright emasculating. And the fact that I'd yet to pick up that jockstrap I mentioned wasn't helping matters, either. After a few pathetic attempts, I headed to the sidelines and struck a sort of bent-knee resting pose I'd noticed other students take when they'd reached their limit, the kung fu equivalent of saying "Screw this crap—I give up."

As I walked home from class that day, the breezy feeling on my downtown real estate suggested that yet another pair of boxers had been sacrificed to the kung fu gods. And what had once been a source of pride had officially become an irritation.

"Another three-pack down the drain," I thought with a sigh as I headed up Broadway in the direction of home while keeping my eyes peeled for a Duane Reade.

I had every intention of returning to class again a couple days later, but after carefully sidestepping my kung fu uniform on my bedroom floor at least a couple hundred times, I suddenly realized it had been weeks since I'd last swung by the temple. Then one day, without even thinking about it, I neatly folded up my kung fu uniform, shoved it into my underwear drawer, and began scouring the Internet for putt-putt courses located within walking distance of my apartment.

THE WORST
ROOMMATE EVER

L IKE A LOT OF SUCKERS, I'D READ SOMEWHERE THAT getting a dog is a good way to figure out if you might be able to handle raising an actual human child one day. And while I'm not entirely opposed to the idea of having or at least acquiring a child somehow at some point, I figured getting a dog might at least be a good way to determine if I might be capable of looking out in any way whatsoever for any living thing other than myself. Plus, getting a dog would make it so that I'd always have someone to hang out and maybe even get a little bit nuts with if none of my friends were around for some reason, so there was that, too.

Keeping all that in mind, I decided to drop a line to my friend Holly, who runs an animal rescue in the East Village. For the past couple years, Holly had been nudging me to adopt or at least foster one of her dogs, and admittedly I had been a bit hesitant. It wasn't because I had never had a dog before, either—I'd had plenty. There was Blazer, a fun-loving golden retriever that bit me in the face when I was eleven, scarring me for life.* There was Chloe, a standoffish chow chow mix my sister Libby had brought home one weekend when my parents were out of town that just seemed to tolerate me at best. And then there was Cain, a massive Rottweiler that lived with me and my sister Miriam for a year, while his owner, my friend Liz, temporarily moved back home with her mother, who preferred the Cain-free lifestyle.

It was just that most of the dogs Holly tried to find homes for seemed to be of the three-legged, one-eyed variety. And while I have no doubt that I would have eventually fallen in love with any of those dogs, too, I tend to be a completist, so it was important to me to have a full dog rather than just some of a dog. I also liked the idea of starting off with a clean slate. That way, if the dog lost an eye or a leg or even both on my watch, it would be *our* story, one we could tell together instead of being some mystery that would rule my thoughts whenever a silence happened to fall between us.

"I sure wish you could talk, little fella," I'd say to my new dog as he squinted up at me with his remaining eye while probably fighting to keep his balance. "I bet you have the craziest stories in the whole wide world, don't cha, buddy?"

But recently Holly had gotten a line on some dogs without any missing parts whatsoever and suggested I have a look at her website to see which ones might be up my alley. I logged on and in-

---

* For further information on this subject, I encourage you to read the essay titled "On Manliness" in my first book, *Tasteful Nudes*, where I go into gory detail about the incident. You know, if you want. No pressure. Whatever.

stantly took a shine to Luke and Lola, two boxer mixes from the same litter.

"No," Holly assured me, "their sister Laurel is the one you really want."

I looked up Laurel on the website only to find a pathetic-looking little mutt with a crazed look in her eye and white spots on her lips that made it look like she had giant fangs her mouth simply couldn't contain. I figured Holly might have been trying to pawn off the ugly one on me since I was a friend and less inclined to fight her on it. But since I was feeling a little guilty about passing on all the one-eyed, three-legged mutts I was talking about earlier, and also figured that if Laurel grew up to be a real looker, it would be fun to talk about how repellent she had been as a puppy, I decided to say yes.

"You can foster her for a week and then you have to let me know whether or not you want to keep her for good," Holly explained.

The idea that I could send Laurel packing after a week if I decided things weren't working out between us made the whole thing all the more appealing.

"Oh, I was just fostering her," I could tell anyone who asked what the hell happened to my new puppy after just one week together, absolving myself of any and all guilt. "It's just my way of, um, giving something back to the dog community."

Laurel would be riding in a van from Tennessee to New York City with Luke, Lola, and a bunch of other dogs the following Saturday, like some sort of canine version of *El Norte*. The problem was, I going to be out of town until Sunday.

"What happens if I don't pick Laurel up Saturday?" I asked.

"Then she'll go back in the van to Tennessee," Holly said with more than a hint of grimness.

The last thing I needed was blood on my hands right out of the gate like that. But fortunately, Holly was able to talk her friend Brittany, who lived a few blocks from me, into hanging on to Laurel until I got back into town. When I returned, I met Brittany on a nearby street corner and she put Laurel, just eight weeks old and shivering from the cold, in my arms in what must have looked to outsiders like the most adorable drug deal ever.

"Hey, little buddy," I whispered into her ear as I slipped her under my coat. "I'm gonna make you the happiest little girl in the world."

It was like something out of one of the better dog-based movies out there today. Even so, I'm not sure either of us was too convinced that she was in particularly good hands. And as Laurel and I headed back through the wind and snow to my place, a mild panic set in. After all, this was the first dog I'd be raising from the ground up, without any parents or siblings to share the load or—perhaps more realistically—manage the load entirely. And, clueless puppy or not, the fact that I'd shown up with a brand-new adult dog–sized collar for her instead of an adorable little puppy-sized one couldn't have given her much confidence that getting out of that van in the first place had been a very good idea.

A few minutes later, Laurel and I were back at my place, where she took a crap in the corner of my living room before I could even get the front door closed.

"Like owner, like dog," I thought, laughing to myself as I thought about all the other humorous jokes like this I'd be able to make in the days or maybe years to come. Then I said "I'm not taking any more shit from you" to Laurel as one more example of that. What with her being a puppy and all, I guess I should have seen the whole taking-a-crap-in-my-living-room thing coming, but somehow it still caught me off guard. And as an unmistakable funk filled the air, I thought back to the puppies that had entered my family's home on two separate occasions when I was a kid. This was usually the point where I'd just walk out of the room, leaving one of my parents or a more responsible sibling to deal with the steaming aftermath.

"Looks like this big boy's all grown up now," I thought as I ran to the kitchen for some paper towels and the nearest bottle of cleanser, ready to handle this situation entirely on my own like a goddamn man.

It was also at that moment that I decided a name change was in order. For whatever reason, Laurel just didn't seem like the right name for the kind of gal who would take a crap in someone's living room without warning like that.

"A Laurel excuses herself," I thought. "A Laurel craps outside like a lady."

So I decided to change Laurel's name to Little Joe Franklin after the legendary talk show host* and friend of mine who had died the week before. It's not that Joe ever struck me as the kind of guy who would take a dump in the corner of someone's living room like that, either. In fact, he was a class act to the core. It just felt like a nice tribute at the time. Still, as great as it sounded

---

* Joe Franklin—if you don't know about him already, look him up. You will thank me.

at first, after a few days of calling my new puppy Little Joe Franklin, it was beginning to feel like a lot of work for both of us. And while I thought I might call her Joe for short, that sounded too much like *no*, another word I had already started using a lot with her, so I crossed that off the list, too.

"Why don't you call her Lucifuge?" my friend Walter suggested reasonably, in reference to the title of the second album by Danzig, which I'd hoped to play a lot for her anyway. According to the popular Wikipedia website, Lucifuge is also the name of the demon in charge of the government in hell, which is awesome. Even so, that felt like a lot of pressure, so I decided to just call her Luci in case the weight of being some sort of weirdly bureaucratic demon was a bit too much for an eight-week-old puppy to handle.

Since Luci was so young and it was still so cold and snowy outside, she spent most of the next few weeks indoors. Fortunately, Carol, a twentysomething law student with a pug named Sparkles, had recently moved into the apartment below me, so a couple times a day I'd let Luci into the hallway to trip up and down the stairs with Sparkles until they'd both be ready to collapse into the most adorable heap of all time.

Meanwhile, up at my place, Luci stayed busy relieving herself wherever and whenever possible, usually when I wasn't looking but also at times seemingly making a point of looking me right in the eye when she did it. It was actually kind of impressive—the second I finished cleaning up one pile of piping-hot puppy poo in the kitchen, she'd serve up a fresh batch in the bedroom, like she was getting paid to do it.

Eventually, Luci would pass out and I'd get at least a short break from the puppy assault, but it never lasted long. The first few nights, I'd be lucky if I slept two hours straight before Luci's yelping would snatch me from my slumber and I'd have to let her out of her crate so that she could take a leak or worse on the carpet mere seconds before I could get her out the apartment door.

"I might as well just get a damn baby while I'm at it," I told my sister Katy, who had also recently gotten a puppy for her two kids.

"A baby is much easier than a puppy at first," Katy said. "I'd rather take care of a baby than a puppy any day."

I was surprised to hear her say that, especially because most people I know with babies act like taking care of them is more stressful than working on the Manhattan Project or something. But the more I thought about it, the more it made sense. After all, until it figures out how to crawl, a baby can only make your life a living hell from one spot. But a puppy can move throughout your entire house right out of the gate, wreaking havoc at every turn, usually without even breaking a stride. It's nuts. The only plus side is that at least you can put a puppy in its cage and leave it home all alone for a couple hours without anyone calling the cops.

Despite the headaches, though, it didn't take long for me and Luci to fall hard for each other, so much, in fact, that even when she'd lick my face and then her butt before trying to lick my face again, I'd just let it happen like it was no big deal at all.

"After all," I thought, "who else will ever love me like this again?"

She might have been a rescue, but most days I couldn't decide whether I rescued Luci or she rescued me. I'm kidding, of course—they were going to kill her before I came along, so there's no question who did the rescuing here—it was definitely me. Under the circumstances, you'd think she would have been a bit more grateful, but as best I could tell Luci didn't give a shit about anything really, at least not in the figurative sense. And when she wasn't busy eating, sleeping, or staining the carpet, she spent the majority of her time biting me.

"She's a puppy," my sister Libby said in the dog's defense. "She's just teething."

Teething or not, the attacks were beginning to feel premeditated and I was losing a lot of blood, so I figured I should do something about it before someone discovered me passed out on the rug.

"Why won't my puppy stop biting me?" I typed into Google.

My query led me to one of those dog whisperer sites.

"The reason your puppy is biting you is because she doesn't respect you as her leader," the dog whisperer explained. "She just sees you as a friend."

Earlier that day Luci had taken a crap on my winter jacket, so I found this answer puzzling. As best I could tell, not only did Luci not respect me as her leader, she didn't respect me *period*. After all, when was the last time you heard of anybody taking a crap on her friend's jacket or any other item of clothing? It just doesn't happen. And the fact of the matter was this four-legged little asshole was really starting to piss me off. Still, there was no denying we were having a lot of fun together. We also had a lot in common. For example, we both love socks, albeit for mostly different reasons. And don't even get me started on how much we both like naps. In fact, as long as I'm on the topic, even though it's kind of gross when Luci rests her head on my chest and conks out with a big exhale that ends up coating my entire face in puppy snot, I'm still kind of weirdly into it. And who cares if she farts like a linebacker? If Luci could talk, she'd be the first to tell you I can give it right back to her if it gets to be too much.

Getting a puppy also had the surprising side effect of at least temporarily relieving me of my daily anxieties. Suddenly, Luci and I were so busy chasing each other around my apartment that I didn't have time to worry about all my usual garden-variety neuroses or the nagging fear of death and how it's coming fast and hard that I let consume my thoughts and dreams. As a result, my weekly therapy sessions quickly turned into hour-long monologues about Luci and all the madcap adventures we'd gotten up to over the past week.

"And then Luci just ran around the living room in a circle like five times for no reason whatsoever!" I'd say to my therapist as he fought with all his might to keep his eyes open. "She's a silly, silly puppy!"

It initially bothered me that I was actually paying for this, but then I realized that anyone forced to listen to someone talk about nothing but his dog for an hour straight deserves every penny.*

One person I figured might actually enjoy hearing about my new dog, though, was my dad—because not only is he a dog lover

---

* The possibility that having to read about someone's dog might be kind of annoying, too, is something that is just now occurring to me. But don't worry—we're nearing the end, you bastard.

himself, but actually getting my own dog after having been maimed by one as a child was a milestone I thought might impress him.

"I got a puppy," I told him during one of our regular phone calls.

"Oh, boy," he replied, sounding not so much enthused as concerned for an innocent animal.

"Want me to bring her to visit?" I asked him.

I figured my dad would be thrilled with this idea, too, but instead he went into some spiel about how they don't allow dogs on his floor at the retirement community or some crap like that before suddenly changing the topic entirely to how he'd been thinking about maybe getting a cat but eventually decided against it because he was either allergic or "too busy for a cat." I can't remember. Regardless, I decided to drag her along with me the next time I went to see him anyway. Luci took a leak on his living room rug, too, something my dad for some reason seemed to think was more my fault than hers, but aside from that, it was a pretty cool hang.

When we got back to New York, I had to go out of town for a few days, so I asked my girlfriend to hold things down with Luci until I got back. By then Luci had grown big enough that Sparkles no longer seemed to enjoy their playdates very much, so my girlfriend and Luci would be forced to make their own Sparkles-free fun together in my absence.

"I haven't even seen Carol or Sparkles in a few days anyway," I told my girlfriend, trying to soften the blow for both of them. "I think they might be out of town."

As best I could tell, Luci and my girlfriend were having a

really great time together until an ungodly stench in my bedroom began to put a damper on things.

"Something in your bedroom is foul," my girlfriend told me. "I think it might be your laundry hamper."

"Sorry about that," I said. "I'll take care of it when I get back."

The next day, the stench was even worse and my girlfriend was officially pissed.

"It's unbearable," she said. "I think it might be coming from underneath the bed."

"I'll be sure to have a look when I get home," I promised her.

"Whatever," she replied. "You're disgusting."

It's not like that was the first time I'd heard that, so I tried not to let it get to me, even after my girlfriend stopped talking to me altogether. After a couple more days, though, she broke her silence.

"Sorry for calling you disgusting," she said. "That smell wasn't your fault, after all."

As it turned out, my girlfriend had run into the building maintenance guy, who told her that apparently Carol had accidentally let Sparkles out of the building without a leash, which resulted in the poor little guy being promptly steamrolled by traffic on nearby Seventh Avenue. Not sure what to do next, Carol carried Sparkles's body back up to her apartment, put it in her bed, and—somehow still not sure what to do next—checked herself into a hotel for the rest of the week. Meanwhile, poor Sparkles spends the next few days rotting below my bedroom, and suddenly *I'm* the disgusting one. Needless to say, it was a huge bummer on several levels, but mostly that one where an adorable little dog ends up getting flattened by a car.

As sad, tragic, and really, really gross as all that was, it at least had the positive side effect of giving me an even firmer resolve to give Luci the best life I possibly could. I mean, sure, I still wanted her to disappear forever at least once a week by now. But c'mon—who in my life *wouldn't* I say that about?

Anyway, to that end (the one about giving her a great life, that is), as soon as I got home, I flipped on the television so that we could spend the rest of the day curled up and watching the Westminster Kennel Club Dog Show together. As you can probably imagine, we were both immediately glued to the screen. Spaniels, pointers, Newfoundlands, terriers, retrievers, even a bichon frise or two—there they all were, scampering about as their tweedy owners walked alongside them, confident in the knowledge that the odds of their perfectly groomed purebred just dropping everything and humping the nearest leg from out of nowhere probably weren't very good at all.

It was hard to tell whether Luci really had a favorite dog or not—if her barking, growling, and whining were any indication, she seemed to have an equal mix of enthusiasm and disdain for all of them. As for me, I couldn't help but have a soft spot for a Shih Tzu named Rocket that just so happened to belong to the famed socialite Patty Hearst. Rocket ended up winning the toy dog category, which was not only thrilling but also just goes to show that everything in life really does happen for a reason. I mean, sure, when Patty was abducted by the Symbionese Liberation Army forty-odd years ago, only to slap on a beret and some military fatigues, grab a rifle, and start robbing banks with those whack jobs, it was just about the craziest thing anyone had ever heard, the seventies equivalent of Paris Hilton joining ISIS or something. But as soon as that Shih Tzu strutted out onto that Astroturf at Madison Square Garden, I couldn't help but think, "Oh, wow—now I totally, *totally* get it."

When Luci first moved in, I came up with a bunch of rules for her I swore would never be broken by either one of us no matter how drunk one of us got. For example, I'd never feed her human food. I'd also never let her in my bed or on any of the furniture. Even so, as I sit here typing this, Luci sits across from me, out cold and drooling on the sofa. I can't stay mad at her, though— once I forget about all the biting, the fact that she uses my entire apartment as her personal restroom, and the seemingly calculated destruction of any of my prized possessions she can get her paws on, I have to admit she's pretty cute. And there is some strange comfort in knowing that in a dozen years or so, this will all be over. And on that day, I will cry like a baby.

I tried to explain this to Luci the other day, but she didn't seem to get it. Instead, she just took a leak in the corner and jumped onto the kitchen table to help herself to some leftover pizza before trying to talk me into a game of fetch with some stuffed thing or another we got at the pet store. It's either an owl or a cat of some sort. Neither of us can really be sure. But dammit if we don't have a lot of fun with that thing. I'll throw it across the living room and she'll bring it back to me over and over again for what seems like hours. And while I think I'd be totally fine having a kid, after all, if he thinks he's ever getting in on any of that action he can just forget about it.

LIKE A ROCKET SLED
ON RAILS

THE BRITISH POET WILLIAM WORDSWORTH ONCE JOTTED down a line somewhere or other that goes "The Child is father of the Man."* And while I have no idea what he meant by that, whenever I hear it, I tend to think of that phenomenon I've often heard about in life where the roles between a child and a parent are reversed, and the child reluctantly stops hitting up his dad for cash and suddenly becomes the caregiver in the relationship.

Aside from maybe asking me to reheat something in the microwave for him every once in a while, my dad and I aren't quite there yet ourselves. Still, it would be a massive understatement to say he's done a lot for me over the years, so it recently occurred to me that I might at least try and return the favor every once in a while, to maybe give a little something back.

---

* It turns out it's in the poem "My Heart Leaps Up." I just looked it up.

But what do you do for a guy who already has a pretty decent cable TV package?

"Dad told me today he's always wanted to drive an eighteen-wheeler," my sister Libby told me over the phone shortly before my dad's eighty-second birthday.

"What?" I asked.

"An eighteen-wheeler, a semi, those big trucks you see on the highway all the time," she reiterated.

"Like the ones that 'Convoy' song is about?" I asked.

"Right," Libby said.

"'Cause we got a mighty convoy rockin' through the night. Yeah, we got a mighty convoy, ain't she a beautiful sight?" I half sung, half said to her. "I love that song."

"Yeah," Libby replied, slightly annoyed. "It's pretty good."

"Who sings that?" I asked.

"I don't know," Libby said firmly. "Anyway, he wants to drive one."*

"B-but I don't understand," I said incredulously, as if I'd just found out my dad had secretly been a member of a satanic cult or a fantasy football league all these years. "Why?"

"I don't know," Libby answered. "He just brought it up from out of nowhere."

My sister and I chatted about my dad's trucking aspirations for a few more minutes before finally dismissing the whole thing

---

* Actually, it's by C. W. McCall and was cowritten with Chip Davis from Mannheim Steamroller. The song was released in 1975, a popular time to be singing about trucks, and spent six weeks at number one on the country charts and one week at number one on the pop charts. And with good reason, too—it is the best song.

as a possible sign of early-onset dementia and hanging up the phone. But when he brought it up again a couple weeks later, we realized the situation was perhaps more serious than we had initially thought.

"Dad was talking about driving a truck again today," Libby called to tell me.

"What did he say this time?" I asked.

"Same thing," Libby replied. "Just that he'd really like to drive one."

It was unsettling news to be sure, not because I have anything against trucking or the trucking lifestyle in general—in fact, everything I'd ever heard about it before sounded great. It's just that this was so out of left field. You think you know someone your whole life and then he springs this on you. "Who is this man?" I wondered. And what other surprises might he have in store? For all I knew, he might ask for a gift card to Jo-Ann Fabrics or want to go folk dancing next or something. I didn't feel safe. In the end, though, I decided that regardless of where this trucking urge might be coming from, if my dad wanted to drive a truck then, dammit, drive a truck he shall. And with that, I called a truck-driving school not far from where my dad lives in an effort to turn his dream into a piston-pumping reality.

"My dad wants to drive an eighteen-wheeler," I told the guy from the truck-driving school, whom I imagined to be wearing a trucker hat and overalls and taking my call from behind the wheel of a massive truck, even though he probably wasn't, the more I think about it right now.

"Tell him to give us a call, then," the guy replied.

"No," I told him. "I want it to be a surprise."

"You want to surprise your dad by sending him to truck-driving school?" the guy asked.

"That would definitely surprise him, but no," I said. "I just want him to be able to drive a truck."

"Well, he's gonna have to take six weeks of classes before he can actually get behind the wheel of a truck," the guy explained.

"You misunderstand me, sir," I said. "He's eighty-two years old and I just want him to be able to drive the truck for a couple minutes just to see what it's like. That's all."

"He'll be able to drive a truck *after* he finishes the first six weeks of classes," the guy replied.

"You heard the part about how my dad is eighty-two, right?" I asked him.

"That doesn't make him any different from anyone else as far as our rules are concerned," the guy answered.

I pleaded with the guy to bend the rules for a few more minutes after that, bringing up stuff like the power of dreams and how I could grease him with a few bucks for helping me out. I even made a humorous joke about how we could make it look like my dad stole the truck if anything went really wrong, but he didn't seem to like it nearly as much as I did. Eventually the bastard just hung up on me altogether.

"No dice," I told my sister later that day. "The guy I spoke to at the truck-driving school said Dad would have to take six weeks of classes before he could drive a truck, and that he needed to start taking things more seriously if he was going to become a truck driver, and blah, blah, blah . . ."

"Well, Dad was talking about trucks some more today," Libby replied.

"He won't shut up about those things," I said.

"I know," Libby said. "It's kind of weird."

"It's definitely weird."

"Anyway, the good news is that he said he'd be satisfied even to just ride in one," Libby replied.

As much I tended to agree with the guy I'd spoken with on the phone that my dad really did need to start taking things more seriously if he was going to become a truck driver, I was relieved to hear things suddenly become a lot more doable. Given my connections in the underworld and also to guys who know guys who drive trucks, I figured I could just make a couple phone calls and my dad would be rolling down the highway in the passenger seat of a big rig in no time, sleeves up, shades on, and wearing an oil-stained mesh cap with something written in puffy, iron-on letters across the front stating the fact that he would rather be fishing or simply engaging in some activity other than the one in which he was presently engaged. Who knows, maybe he'd even be allowed to work the horn.

"This is going to be really, really great," I thought. "I'm a good son."

Before I had a chance to sort any of this out on my own, though, my sister called another truck-driving school in town that was willing to let my dad ride shotgun in an eighteen-wheeler with one of their instructors totally free of charge and made plans for us to visit the following weekend.

In an effort to completely blow his mind right out of his skull, we decided not to tell my dad where we were going on the day of his maiden voyage. Instead, I told him we were meeting Libby and her son, Blake, on the other side of town and he should just get in the car and not to ask any goddamn questions. Since, at eighty-two, he's lucky to make it more than a few blocks from his apartment most days, he just rolled with it.

It was hard figuring what else to talk about besides where exactly I might be taking him on the drive over, but somehow we managed and, after about forty-five minutes, my dad and I finally pulled into the parking lot of the truck-driving school. He seemed mildly confused at first, but I could tell he was pretty pumped in general at what might possibly happen next. I parked the car and we walked inside the truck-driving school to find Libby and Blake waiting for us in the lobby.

"You're gonna go for a ride in a truck!" Libby told my dad with a hug.

"That's great," my dad said, and smiled, trying to play it cool.

The lobby of the truck-driving school was decorated in a mixture of taxidermy and photos of trucks, just as you might expect. As we stood there, taking in the majesty of it all, a lady from the truck-driving school came over to tell us that the instructor wasn't quite ready to hit the road yet, so we should just take a seat and enjoy the magazines on display, most of which were about trucking and the trucking lifestyle, which was awesome. One magazine even rated the best cities to live in if you're a trucker, though I couldn't bring myself to look at it for fear of having to move. At one point, I excused myself to use the restroom, and when I returned, I learned that in my absence my nephew Blake had been given a tour of the entire school by someone on the staff, which is bullshit, since I am way more into truck driving than he'll ever be in a million trillion years, but whatever.

"I saw the classrooms where the truck-driving teachers teach the truck-driving students about truck driving," he told me, trying to rub it in. I tried not to let it get to me too much.

After a few more minutes, a guy named Steve with a gray beard and wearing jean shorts, a neon-green sleeveless T-shirt, a baseball cap, and spotless white sneakers roared up to the front of the school in a massive eighteen-wheeler, leaving an impressive trail of dust in his wake. Then he hopped out and stood proudly in front of the truck with his arms folded like he was in the opening credits of some awesome show about truck drivers that existed entirely in his mind.

"That's your man," the lady at the truck-driving school told us, waving us outside. I hadn't seen my dad move that fast since the eighties—it was as if he were fleeing a burning building. Part of me worried for his safety, but it was also nice to see what he was capable of when he really put his mind to it.

"Welcome aboard!" Steve told us as he kicked a few empty Big Gulps out of the way so that we could pile in more easily. "Sorry about the trash."

Predictably, my dad called shotgun, so Libby, Blake, and I piled into the spacious cabin just behind the driver's seat, an area I had initially thought to be reserved solely for sex, but apparently suitable for additional seating in a pinch.

"That's where the students ride when I'm showing them the ropes," Steve explained, as if I didn't know better.

It turned out Steve was seventy-one years old, which made him a mere child as far as my dad was concerned, but even so, the two of them managed to close the gap between their years and hit it off instantly, just a couple of dudes sitting in the front seat of a big rig together like they were born to do it.

As we pulled out into the road, Steve began to explain the inner workings of the truck to my dad.

"This, of course, is the gearshift," he said, slapping his palm on top of a big lever sticking out of the control panel. My dad just nodded knowingly, as if to say, "What else you got?" It was like he had been waiting for this moment his whole life.

After a couple of blocks, Steve pulled onto the highway to show us what his rig could really do and a big smile slowly spread across my dad's face. I couldn't help but smile a little, too, as the feeling of barreling down the road at sixty-five miles per hour–plus in this mighty machine was downright exhilarating. Since I didn't want to spoil the moment for my dad, though, I did my best not to emit any high-pitched noises or anything and just kept quiet in the back as he and Steve engaged in a bit of guy talk, mostly stuff about the unions, something called a "lot lizard," and another thing about how the road can be a "cruel mistress."

"You know what they say, Bob," Steve told my dad as he continued nodding along. "What happens on the road stays on the road."

It ruled.

I had assumed our truck ride might take about ten minutes, but it ended up lasting over an hour and a half, which initially felt like a really long time for the four of us to be driving around in a truck with some guy in jean shorts named Steve we'd just met. But then suddenly it hit me—sometimes in life an eighteen-wheeler is just going to come along when you least expect it and you've got no choice but to climb aboard and ride in that damn thing wherever it might take you. And if you end up having to go to the bathroom or something at any point, you can always just grab your nephew's Gatorade bottle. What's he gonna do about it? You are much bigger and stronger than he is. Also, after that momentary panic that Steve was some sort of lunatic kidnapping us in his semi and taking us to the woods to start a new life for ourselves as members of a secret, truck-loving community entirely immune to the rules of decent society, Libby, Blake, and I managed to really settle in and enjoy the ride at least half as much as my dad appeared to be.

"You want me to take one last lap before I let you out?" Steve asked as he finally pulled back into the trucking school parking lot.

"No, thank you!" I blurted before my dad had a chance to answer. "We're good!"

Despite the more than ample amount of time we'd spent in that truck, it took a bit of coaxing to get my dad to finally get out of the passenger seat and into my rental car for the ride home. And as I waited for that to happen, I thanked Steve for our joyride by slipping him a couple twenties when no one was looking, something I mention merely to point out that I do cool shit like that all the time and it's not a big deal at all.

As my dad and I headed down the road back toward his place, a peaceful silence fell between us, the kind that I'm guessing can only be attained after riding around aimlessly in an eighteen-wheeler together for nearly two hours straight. It was pretty cool.

As if a ride in an eighteen-wheeler weren't enough, also on the docket for us that weekend was a ninety-eighth-birthday party for my aunt Helen. And as we sat in a semicircle around Aunt Helen the following afternoon, bingeing on ham sandwiches, potato salad, and cake with green frosting in acknowledgment of her Irishness, and other standard ninety-eighth-birthday-party accoutrements, my dad regaled anyone who would listen about his trucking escapade the day before.

"I got to ride in the front seat and everything," my dad said proudly as Aunt Helen quietly looked on, nodding politely at my dad, this kid in her eyes, who wouldn't shut the hell up about trucks.

"I think everyone really liked my truck story," my dad said as we headed back to his place a couple hours later.

"Definitely," I replied, keeping my eyes on the road ahead. "It really does have everything."

I was scheduled to fly back to New York the following afternoon, so the next morning my dad and I woke early to head into town for breakfast at a local diner, where he somehow managed to corner the owner of the place long enough to tell him all about the truck ride, too.

"Trucks are pretty cool," the guy said while scanning the restaurant for something, anything else that might immediately require his attention.

"Yup," my dad agreed before returning to his eggs. "They sure are."

When we got back to his place afterward, I decided to go for a quick run in the woods across the street from his place.

"I've gotta go to my book club at noon," my dad told me as I laced up my running shoes. "In case I'm already gone before you get back, it was good to see you."

"Good to see you, too, Dad," I said before heading out the door.

I'm not sure how far I ran that day as, even a couple days after riding in that truck, the diesel fumes were still getting to me and time and space remained in the abstract. Regardless, at one point I looked at my phone to see it was closing in on noon. And though we'd already said our good-byes, I suddenly felt the urge to race back to my dad's place in hopes of catching him before he left.

When I got back to his retirement community, I spotted my dad already in the parking lot, slowly making his way toward his Buick, slightly hunched over, cane in hand, and wearing an old tan blazer I remember borrowing from him back in high school, when my dad and I were about the same size. I was stunned how small he looked to me in that moment, maybe even a bit frail. Perhaps for the first time in my life, he suddenly looked not just like the same old dad I'd known all these years but also like the old man that he is, the guy I imagine strangers must see when they see him walking down the street.

"Dad!" I called out as I galloped toward him.

He stopped, looked up, and smiled at me as I continued my approach. When I finally met him, drenched in sweat and panting heavily, I felt like a towering beast compared to him.

"Thanks again for that truck ride, Dave," my dad told me, shaking my hand.

"Anytime," I said.

"I'm proud of you," he then said. "I'm not sure if I ever told you that before."

"Thanks," I replied, not sure, either.

Then he slowly climbed into his Buick, fired up the engine, and headed down the road as I disappeared in his rearview mirror.

Later that day, on the flight back to New York, I began to

think about why my dad wanted to ride in that truck so badly in the first place. Maybe the truck somehow represented a different path in life to him, one entirely different from the one he had chosen where he joined the Army, became a lawyer, married my mom, and spent the rest of his life working hard to provide for me and my siblings, making countless sacrifices for us every step of the way. Still, despite this relatively conventional lifestyle, his love, for example, of art, music, and literature was no secret. And when I began to take an interest in those same things as a kid, it was he who helped me get started, drawing military generals and other subjects of interest I would then closely copy myself, loaning me the beat-up old nylon-stringed guitar he'd bought shortly after getting out of the Army so that I might learn a few chords before I begged him to buy me one of my own, and even offering to help with writing assignments I'd been given in school.

"I like that you do a lot of the stuff I would have liked to do if I hadn't decided to settle down and have a family," my dad told me a couple of years ago in a moment of weakness, perhaps after having taken too much cold medicine or something.

Up until that point, it had never really occurred to me that my dad ever considered making a career out of any of those things. And it was at that moment that I realized maybe we weren't so different, after all—we had just made different choices in life. Now knowing this, I began to make a point of calling him from wherever in the world my own work ended up taking me—be it Australia, Germany, England, Japan, or even the wilds of lower Ontario—so that we might, if only for a moment, be able to enjoy these experiences together.

"I always thought it would be neat to be a touring jazz musician," he once told me during an expensive international call that I was totally paying for, "so I like that I sort of get to experience it vicariously through you."

Keeping that in mind, my dad's trucking itch suddenly began to make a bit of sense. Maybe all this stuff was somehow connected. After all, there's an undeniable freedom that goes with hitting the open road in a massive truck, tearing along the highway at breakneck speed for miles and miles at a time while sucking on a Marlboro and dragging a trailer full of God knows what behind you as the rest of the world slowly fades into the distance. And now that my dad was on his own again for the first time in almost fifty years, perhaps the urge to connect with that side of himself once more, however symbolically, could no longer be denied. The more I thought about it, the more I found it actually kind of inspiring.

Once I got back to my apartment in New York, I decided to give him a ring to see how close I might have actually been about all that.

"So, Dad, what made you want to go for a ride in an eighteen-wheeler so badly anyway?" I asked him.

"Years ago your mother and I stayed in a motel in New Jersey one night," he began. "And in the parking lot there were these big eighteen-wheelers, so I decided to step outside to get a closer look at them."

There was a long pause after this, during which I assumed my dad was simply giving me a moment to brace myself before he completely blew my mind.

"And?" I said, urging him on.

"Well," he said, "they're just so bright and shiny."

ACKNOWLEDGMENTS

Books—will we ever really understand them? Probably not. But one thing I can tell you for certain is this book would not have been possible without all the people I am about to mention in an effort to fulfill my contractually agreed-upon word count. I mean, sure, I did all the writing, which is the hard part, but trust me on this one— there's other stuff, too. And while I will no doubt forget some people who deserve to be mentioned here, please know that this is completely unintentional with the exception of Harry Deansway, whom I am once again leaving out on purpose and aggressively so.

Anyway, for starters, I would like to thank the fine folks at Blue Rider Press, especially David Rosenthal, who, it is my understanding, came up with the cash, and, of course, my editor Sarah Hochman, whose patience, insight, and dedication to this project from its crude beginnings as a handful of dick jokes scribbled down on the back of a parking ticket to the American classic it is today is something for which I am eternally grateful. I also think it was really cool that you always let me order whatever I wanted at restaurants and paid *every single time* without complaint, even when I ordered extra stuff to go. This is the definition of grace.

I would also like to thank my agent, Kirby Kim. From my humble beginnings on the sandlots of the Dominican Republic straight on up to the big leagues, you have stuck with me every step of the way. Thank you for repeatedly talking people into giving me money. That is so cool. I still say the 50/50 split you claim is standard is kind of weird, but whatever—you're the pro, I guess.

I am forever grateful to my manager, Kara Welker. You are the best at managing and about five hundred other things, too. And all these years later, the fact that you carry a knife everywhere is something I still think is so, so awesome. There is a space between terrified and exhilarated, and that is where I live.

A gigantic thanks goes to my lovely and talented secretary, Shaina Feinberg, for reading and rereading these pages and helping me decide exactly where the F-bombs should and should not go, all while having a human baby. We nailed it.

A big thanks also goes to the many friends, family members, and assorted other fine folks who, whether they realize it or not, gave me the support, focus, distraction, and love required to complete what is seriously the best book the more I sit here thinking about it. They are, in largely random order, Kathy Kato, Libby Manthei, Miriam Hill, Bob Hill (my brother, not my dad, which is different), Katy Wallace, Janyce Murphy, Anna Hill, Eamon Hill, Jeff Manthei, Blake Manthei, Nick Simon, Luke Simon, Rob Wallace, William Wallace, Lilah Wallace, Dick Cavett, Carl Arnheiter, Kieran Blake, Adam Resnick, Fred Wistow, Dan Dratch, Phil Costello, John Herguth, Malcolm Gladwell, Mike Sacks, Chris Lee, Sean Yseult, Todd Barry, Rich Fulcher, Janeane Garofalo, Danielle Velarde, Chris Elliott, John Kimbrough, Bridget Everett, Eric Gilliland, Lucifuge,

ACKNOWLEDGMENTS

Danne D, Sheila Kenny, Tim Parnin, Bob and Barb Kato, Martin Beyer-Olsen, Will and Julie Tanous, Jim McPolin, Michael Heaton, Ali Rushfield, Andy Richter, Rob Pfeiffer, Tim Fornara, Eddie Eyeball, Ira Glass and the *This American Life* folks, Billy Nord, Rebecca O'Malley, Damien Echols, Carmine Street Guitars, Jim Gaffigan, Tom Papa, Lars Berrum, Patrick Salt Ryan, Shifu Shi Yan Ming, Simon Doonan, Laraine Newman, Joe Manning, Gustavo Haelin Hernandez Zertuche, Philip Anselmo, Kelly Oxford, Kate Richardson, Pat Casa, Tony Kellers, Bob Coogan, the Laurent-Marke family, Joe Franklin, Dr. Walter Nosal, Greg Wands, Michael Ian Black, Mike IX Williams, Trish Nelson, the University Heights Police Department, Diana St. John, Korri Santillan, Mel Robbins, Fran Illgen, Pete Sedlac, Rich Woodson, Officer Bartos, Jodi Lennon, Greg Schneider, Grounded Coffee, Chenoa Estrada, Tony Faske, Scott Guber, Rob Pasbani and Metal Injection, Sandy Mullin, Brooklyn Vegan, WFMU, Lou Hagood, Big Gay Ice Cream, and Joe Randazzo, the streetest guy I know probably.

Finally, I would like to thank my mom, Bernadette Hill. I love you and miss you every day. And, of course, my dad, Robert W. Hill, Sr. Please know I tried to keep the profanity to a minimum this time around and only really used it in instances when it would have been totally weird not to. I love you and hope you'll understand.

Oh, and I almost forgot to thank you, the reader. I really appreciate your reading this book and hope you enjoyed it so much. And if you didn't, the joke is on you because I just tricked you into reading until the very end anyway.

Your man,
Dave Hill

ABOUT THE AUTHOR

Dave Hill is a comedian, writer, and musician originally from Cleveland but now living in New York City. He has written for *The New York Times*, *The Paris Review*, *Salon*, *GQ*, *McSweeney's*, the *Cleveland Plain Dealer*, the New York *Daily News*, and *Guitar World*, among other publications. He is a regular contributor to public radio's *This American Life* and hosts his own radio show, *The Goddamn Dave Hill Show*, on WFMU in Jersey City, New Jersey. Dave has starred in his own TV series, *The King of Miami*, on the MOJO Network. He has also appeared on Comedy Central, BBC America, MTV, and Adult Swim, among others, and is a regular host on HBO and Cinemax. Dave performs live comedy in theaters and basements all over the world. He also plays guitar and sings in his own rock band, Valley Lodge, whose song "Go" is the theme song for HBO's *Last Week Tonight with John Oliver*. *Dave Hill Doesn't Live Here Anymore* is his second collection of nonfiction essays. *Tasteful Nudes: . . . and Other Misguided Attempts at Personal Growth and Validation* is his first.